CW00525837

VISHAL M

Vishal Mangalwadi is active in evangelism, politics, and agricultural development in India. With his wife Ruth, he founded the Association for Comprehensive Rural Assistance (ACRA) in 1976, and started medical, agricultural, educational and evangelistic programmes as well as cottage industry projects to generate employment for peasants in rural India. As the work grew, it began to be perceived as a threat by political and financial vested interests. Opposition to the work included arrests and murder threats, and the burning down of ACRA property. 'As I became aware that poverty was planned and perpetuated by powerful people,' writes the author, 'my emphasis changed from development to reform.'

Vishal Mangalwadi is also the author of *The World of Gurus* and *Dear Rajan – Letters to a New Believer*.

SPIRE

By the same author

Dear Rajan – Letters to a New Believer
The World of Gurus

Vishal Mangalwadi

TRUTH AND SOCIAL REFORM

Copyright © 1989 by Vishal Mangalwadi

First published in Great Britain 1989
First published by Nivedit Good Books, Delhi

Spire is an imprint of Hodder and Stoughton Publishers

British Library Cataloguing in Publication Data
Mangalwadi, Vishal
Truth and social reform.
1. Politics,—Christian viewpoints
I. Title
261.7
ISBN 0-340-42630-6

Printed in Great Britain for Hodder and Stoughton Limited, Mill Road, Dunton Green, Sevenoaks, Kent by Richard Clay Limited, Bungay, Suffolk. Photoset by Rowland Phototypesetting Limited, Bury St Edmunds, Suffolk.

Hodder and Stoughton Editorial Office: 47 Bedford Square, London WC1B 3DP.

To
the supporters of TEAR Fund
who care
THANK YOU

CONTENTS

INTRODUCTION

The discovery of truth is explosive, because it calls for major changes in our outlook and service. I hope that will be a liberating, not a frightening, experience. One basic assumption of the Protestant Reformation – one of the greatest reform movements of all times – was that because the Bible is God's objective revelation to man, each individual can read it and know the truth, without blind submission to the Church's infallible interpretation and traditions. If my interpretations appear to be iconoclastic, it is because (a) I am going away from some of our traditional understandings, back to the Word of God and (b) because I assume that the Bible speaks not to our souls, to give us some religious experience, but to the real world. A world that is really fallen, but can be reformed.

Three trillion dollars have been spent, since the Second World War, in the effort to 'develop' the poor of the Third World. The results, however, have been minimal. Since 1976, my wife, Ruth, and I have had the privilege of being involved with the development scene on the front line. This experience both shattered our illusion that there is any easy answer to poverty, and gave insights into the application of Scriptures to socio-economic realities.

Truth and Social Reform discusses poverty in the context of the supernatural dimension of reality. It presents biblical insights gained in the heat of experience, in the hope that it will enrich the reader's understanding of Christian faith and service wherever he or she may live and serve.

Vishal Mangalwadi
March 1989

1

COMPASSION AND SOCIAL REFORM: JESUS THE TROUBLEMAKER

Compassion for the suffering individual and concern for the glory of God were undoubtedly the prime motives of Christ's service. But if compassion had meant for Christ merely what most Christians understand by it today, then Jesus would never have been killed. He would have been a fit candidate for a Nobel prize, not the cross.

Christ's compassion was prophetic. Instead of being a gut-level response to pictures of starving children, it grew out of a prophetic insight into the social and theological causes of suffering. In His response, therefore, Jesus went to the root of human misery and dealt with it. In this chapter we shall look at three facets of Christ's compassion and service which led to His death. In an earlier age, when Protestants still believed in social protest, such a commentary would have been redundant. But today? Well, we have drifted so far from our Biblical and historical heritage, that it may seem too radical to some people.

Service: A Stirring of a Stagnant Pool

In John 5, Jesus healed a man who had been sick for thirty-eight years. The lame man was lying near a pool of water. When the waters of the pool were stirred, therapeutic powers went into action and the sick who entered the water were healed. This was not superstition, but something the man had been witnessing for decades. If he hadn't seen the healing powers of those waters, he wouldn't have stayed there for all those years. He was sick. The treatment was free and within his sight, yet he could not get to it. Why not? He explained to Jesus that he did not have anyone who would put him into the water when it was stirred. No one cared for him.

Jesus asked him to pick up his mat and walk. He did. And it was the Sabbath. In Israel, you could forget whether it was Tuesday or Thursday, but no one ever forgot it was the Sabbath.

Their society was so well organised that in no time the Jewish authorities knew that this unknown man had dared to break the Sabbath rule; he had picked up his bed and was walking. An on-the-spot enquiry began. How efficient! Was it the beauty of that society? No, an establishment which didn't care for a man for thirty-eight years was prompt in caring for its own inhuman rules. I find it hard to believe that they were so keen to enforce the Sabbath legislation because they wanted to please God. I am more inclined to think that their real interest was to impose a fine and collect a little extra revenue! The sick man had complained to Jesus that his problem was that the Jewish society had no compassion. It hadn't even bothered to enforce a basic etiquette of civilised behaviour – 'first come first served'. The resourceful came late, but got healed first.

It was not by mistake that Jesus asked this powerless man to challenge an inhuman society by a deliberate act of defiance of its rule. God had provided the stirred-up pool of water for the healing of this man. It was the social pool of a stagnant, selfish society that needed to be stirred up for the healing of men like him. That was precisely what Jesus did. He not only healed the man, but also asked him to break the Sabbath rule, which led to an attempt by the Establishment on Jesus's life (John 5:18).

Does the healing ministry of the Church today, even its community health work, lead to such retaliation from society? No, because our service does not touch the real issue at all. Many sick men, women and children in the villages and slums of my country die daily, not because treatment is not available or is expensive, but simply because no one cares to take the treatment to them. In some of the villages in my district, young women die during childbirth, simply because their villages are marooned for two to three months during the monsoon. Our society builds flyovers on streets in Delhi because the élite cannot stop for two minutes at red lights, but we are not bothered about those who have no access to any treatment for three months almost every year.

The Establishment plans for the Olympic Games to be held in India; it plans for colour TV; it can send satellites to the sky, but it cannot take simple sanitation to the dying destitutes in its slums. The Church says it cares, yet so often it does not dare to expose the selfishness of the élite which is the real cause of the hundreds of basic diseases which should have been wiped out by now, if only clean water, adequate sanitation, adequate nutrition, health education and immunisation were made available to the poor masses. The technology and financial resources are available in abundance for taking these services to the poor. Yet they starve, suffer and die because the powerful have other priorities. Christ's mercy did not touch the individual alone. It sought to touch the heart of a society. It sought to awaken the sleeping conscience of society. It troubled the stagnant waters which brought about a torrent of retaliation from vested interests.

Service: A Judgment of a Blind Society

After He opened the eyes of a beggar who was born blind (John 9), Jesus did not suggest He was a 'servant'. He said, 'I came to this world to judge, so that the blind should see and those who see should become blind' (John 9:39 GN).

The disciples asked Jesus, 'Rabbi, who sinned, this man or his parents, that he was born blind?'

This question seems to have hurt Jesus. It is hard to

believe that the disciples were asking a sincere question about the cause of an inexplicable suffering. Certainly Jesus did not think that they had a profound philosophical interest in the problem of suffering which deserved an answer. Were the disciples really asking, 'Rabbi, could you kindly provide us with some good rationale to justify our indifference to the suffering of this man?'

True, the man was born blind. But did he have to be a beggar? True, both he and his parents were sinners. But was Israel justified in ignoring the fact that he was also a human being made in the image of God, worthy of love and care? He was begging, neither because he was blind, nor because he was a sinner, but because Israel was blind to the fact that he was an image-bearer of God, the crown of God's creation. He was a beggar because Israel had sinned by not caring for him. Instead of seeing their own sinful indifference the disciples were more keen on finding out his sin and that of his parents.

Jesus, therefore, sought to open their eyes by His brilliant act of civil disobedience.

The incident in John 5 was not an isolated happening. It was part of Christ's pattern. On that occasion Jesus had simply asked the sick man to break the Sabbath law. Then in chapter 9 He did it Himself. In order to open the eyes of this blind man, He did not need to spit on the ground and make mud with the spit, especially on a Sabbath day when He knew that it would be seen as 'work' and therefore a deliberate act of defiance of the Establishment's laws. Yet, He did it. It was a deliberate provocation of the Establishment. Jesus also asked the blind man to break the law, 'Go and wash your face in the pool of Siloam' (John 9:7 GN). Jesus did not need to do this in order to heal him, but healing him was not the only objective of Christ's service. His objective included exposing the blindness of the self-righteous Establishment and condemning it publicly. Had not God commanded Israel in the Old Testament to have mercy on its poor? If Israel was righteous and obedient, why did this man beg on the streets in order to live?

Civil disobedience is a deliberate and courageous act of a reformer to expose and condemn the institutionalised evils of his day. That is what Jesus was doing. And the Establishment was blind enough to be thus exposed. Instead of containing Christ's service by patronising it, they condemned the healing of a blind man, simply because it was done on a Sabbath. They excommunicated the man from the synagogue and thereby further exposed their own blindness. The world was able to see that a mighty prophet had arisen among them who could open the eyes of a man born blind, yet the Establishment could see nothing more than the violation of its own petty rules. Its values, its ideals, its attitudes, its priorities all stood exposed and condemned. The world was able to see that its rulers did not care for their people, but Christ did. The sheep were able to perceive that Jesus was their true shepherd who dared to stand against the wolves pretending to be their custodians.

Jesus made the blind man pay a heavy price for his healing. He was excommunicated from the synagogue because he chose to speak the truth. No doubt, he would have been welcomed into the community of Christ's disciples, yet his excommunication must have helped many sincere Jews to make up their minds against their own rulers whose own blindness had been exposed.

Such service which judges the world is not pleasant. The authorities not only excommunicated the man; they also made it known publicly that Jesus was persona non grata. Whoever said that Jesus was Christ would be excommunicated. It became harder to associate with Jesus; being seen around Him could land someone into trouble.

The Association for Comprehensive Rural Assistance (ACRA) is the community with which I served the rural poor in Chattarpur district of Madhya Pradesh from 1976 till April 1983. We were involved in service which stirred the social pool, which judged the blindness of the Establishment. When you judge the world, the world retaliates by judging you. During May 1982, thirty of us were

arrested on four different occasions, because we not only
helped the victims of a hail-storm, but also through
our service exposed the insensitivity of the politicians
towards the victims of this natural calamity. The politicians not only had us arrested, but they also tried to have
me murdered. The superintendent of police himself
threatened this. Many Christian leaders were frightened,
and disassociated themselves from me. Such treatment
hurts. It makes you lose friends. They choose not to
associate with you, lest they, too, get into trouble. Yet, one
has to decide whether he wishes to walk in the footsteps of
his Master and serve the oppressed, or please his friends.
Jesus's mercy did not touch a blind beggar alone. How
many blind could He heal in three years anyway? How
many blind can the Church heal through its hospitals and
eye centres? We must have compassion for the individual.
But we must also understand that he is a beggar not
because he is blind, but because the society in which he
lives is blind to his need. A blind man can be happy and
fulfilled if society cares for him.

Karl Marx rightly understood that true compassion
calls for dealing with the social context which makes men
miserable. Marx, however, defeated his own purpose by
trying to build a case for compassion on atheistic premises.
If the individual man is merely a product of random
chance in an impersonal universe, then there is no meaning in caring for him, especially when he is too weak and
powerless to be of any use to us. But if man is a created
being, then he is special to his Creator. If he is created as
the image-bearer of the Creator Himself, he is even more
special. If each individual is to relate to the Creator in an
intimate personal relationship and to carry out His will
for Him in this world, then he is very special indeed. That
is how Jesus saw this blind beggar. 'He is blind so that
God's power might be seen at work in him' (John 9:3 GN).

Because an 'unknown' blind beggar is special to God we
must have compassion for him individually. This compassion must be visible in specific acts of mercy, but our

compassion for him must go deep enough to create a society which can see that a beggar is a special person for God; he ought not to be allowed to destroy his self-respect by begging. He should not have to live a hand-to-mouth insecure existence, until one day he falls sick, becomes too weak to beg and rots by the roadside to be eaten by beasts, birds and worms.

If our society cannot see that a blind beggar is a special person, then we are blind to truth. And if we do not acknowledge our blindness, then we are hypocritical, self-righteous and sinful. We should condemn the blindness of our society, and work to build a more humane and compassionate community within it.

Service: An Alternative Power for Social Change

It is not enough to stir a society or to judge a blind Establishment. If the leadership does not repent, if it does not decide to fulfil its responsibility, then it becomes our task to seek to provide an alternative. Servanthood is the Biblical means of acquiring power to lead. However, if it becomes known that the purpose of our service is to change the status quo, to change the leadership, then we are in trouble. The final decision to kill Jesus was made by the Jewish authorities after He raised Lazarus from the dead (John 11), and when He began to be seen popularly as a shepherd, Messiah and king.

Jesus loved Lazarus and his sisters Mary and Martha. These sisters sent word to Him that Lazarus, His beloved friend, was sick. Jesus could have healed him by a word from wherever He was and saved the sisters from much agony. But no; His healing ministry had purposes other than mere healing. He waited till Lazarus died. He waited till the Jews in Jerusalem heard of his death and had assembled in his village, Bethany, to comfort his sisters. Then, in front of a crowd, Jesus displayed His love for the dead man and his sisters. Jesus displayed His sorrow and anger at sickness and death which caused such anguish to His beloved. Jesus displayed His unique relationship with God, His Father, and He displayed His authority and power to give life to the dead.

This display of love, sorrow, anger and power were the means of exhibiting who He really was, so that people could make an intelligent choice for or against Him. Jesus's prayer in John 11:41–2 makes it abundantly clear that even though Jesus could have healed Lazarus and raised him from the dead without exhibiting who He was, He felt it necessary at that point to enable the world to see His heart, His being and His power.

The miracle had the intended effect: many people believed in Jesus. Their choice of Jesus was an automatic rejection of the Establishment (John 12:9–11). Jesus had provided an alternative to Israel and people began to accept it. The Jewish Establishment was aligned to the exploitative Roman regime (John 19:15). It existed because it not only allowed but also enabled Rome to continue its exploitation of the people. The chief priests knew that if Jesus was allowed to extend His influence over the people, a new centre of mass power would be created which would be in the interest of the common man. Rome obviously could not tolerate a leadership which defended the interest of the people. Therefore, it was inevitable that 'the Roman authorities will take action and destroy our Temple and our nation' (John 11:48). Therefore, if the nation was to be 'saved' the shepherd had to be eliminated (John 11:49–50). Slavery is better than destruction was their rationale.

The healing ministry of Jesus was intended not merely to heal but to build up a mass following, just as His preaching was aimed not merely at educating but also at drawing out a whole-hearted dedication to follow Him. The separation of evangelism and church planting has created a mentality among Christians all over the world which leads to preaching and serving, but not to building up a following. Because of this mentality many people cannot even see in the Gospel the obvious fact that Jesus was building up a disciples-based movement through His teaching, preaching and healing.

However, a fresh look at the Gospels will convince the reader that Jesus carefully built a large following which was not just another religious sect, but was an alternative centre of power in Israel. It was a threat to the status quo not only naturally, but also intentionally, because it was the very antithesis of all the Establishment represented.

First, this alternative centre of power was a moral force in contrast to the immoral Jewish Establishment. Jesus had not only healed men but also called them to 'stop sinning' (John 5:14). He called His disciples to righteousness which 'surpasses that of the Pharisees and the teachers of the law' (Matt. 5:20).

Second, it was a social force that stood for the smallest of men in contrast to the Establishment which protected the interests of the powerful exploiters such as the traders in the temple whom Jesus called robbers (Mark 11:15–18). Jesus called His followers to serve 'the least important ones', the hungry, the naked, the sick, the homeless, the prisoners (Matt. 25:31–46).

Third, this alternative power was a courageous force. It required a determination to stand for the protection of the harassed and helpless sheep to the point of the laying down of one's own life (John 10:1–12). This was a contrast to the Jewish Establishment which was concerned primarily for its own safety and well-being, and in the face of the Roman threat was prepared to sacrifice the interest of the common man (John 11:45–8).

Jesus intentionally built up His following, His Church, as a power structure to withstand the mighty forces of destruction and death. He said to Peter, '. . . you are Peter and on this rock I will build my church, and the gates of Hades will not overcome it' (Matt. 16:18). The destructive forces of death will fight against Christ's new society, but will not prevail against it. The Church was meant to stand against the forces of oppression and death because it was asked to 'feed my lambs' and 'take care of my sheep'. In an unjust, oppressive society when a group stands up for the smallest of lambs, it automatically stands up against the mighty vested interests which grow fat on their flesh.

Jesus and His new community were naturally and intentionally a threat to the Establishment then. When Jesus set His face to go to Jerusalem and precipitate a confrontation, the Establishment had to choose between its own survival and the status quo on the one hand, and a titanic socio-political change and transfer of power to another group on the other hand.

Even though it is true that, in many cases, the 'Sunday-school Jesus' confines Himself only to the changing of men's hearts, the Jesus of the Gospels aimed at changing both human hearts and human society. He prepared shepherds to replace wolves from the leadership of Israel. He made His intentions explicit. For example, in the parable of the labourers in the vineyard (Matt. 21:31–46), He concluded by telling the chief priests, 'And so I tell you that the kingdom of God will be taken away from you and given to a people who will produce the proper fruits' (v.43).

Here was an explicit statement of a radical social transformation, of change of political power. The Jews understood it and tried to arrest Him on the spot, but they were afraid of the crowds, who considered 'Jesus to be a prophet' (v.46). Jesus announced His intention of a social change to the Establishment itself after He had carefully built up His mass support, even though the wise men had announced His kingship at His birth and John the Baptist had announced some of the changes that Jesus was to bring about before Jesus began His work. Jesus asserted His royal authority over Zion, through the dramatic events of His triumphal entry into Jerusalem on Palm Sunday, only after the raising of Lazarus, which had created an excitement in the masses.

Power was not an accidental by-product of service. It never is. The Church has no real competitor in the field of service in India today. But it continues to be powerless. This is because our service is very different from Christ's. He consciously cultivated a mass following. Jesus was a man of the masses and He built up His massive following by His service. Look at His strategy following the raising of Lazarus in John's Gospel (John 11:45–12:33).

First, He brought a dead man back to life. He allowed the story of this fantastic miracle to spread to the point when it started ringing alarm-bells in the ears of the Establishment (John 11:45–53). Then, He withdrew to a desert town, Ephraim (v.54). It was the time of the Passover festival, therefore many Jews poured into Jerusalem. They naturally gossiped about Jesus (11:55–7); after He had become the hot topic of debate, He returned to Bethany, to Lazarus' home, just two kilometres from Jerusalem; the word spread in Jerusalem and crowds flocked, to see not only Him but also Lazarus (John 12:1–11). Then, when a large enough crowd had gathered about Jesus, He asked for a colt and allowed His disciples to organise a procession. They marched into Jerusalem proclaiming Him to be the King of Israel. The whole city was stirred up, until the authorities sat up and said to each other, 'You see, we are not succeeding at all! Look, the whole world is following him' (John 12:19).

The result of this strategy was that the Jews decided to kill both Jesus and Lazarus (John 12:9–11). Christ knew that this would be the consequence of what He was doing, but He had no choice. The Establishment had refused to repent; it had refused to believe the truth and had decided to continue in its evil ways. Either Jesus had to give up His call for repentance and change or He had to precipitate a confrontation to give a last opportunity to the Establishment either to repent or to kill Him. Jesus was prepared to pay the price of such a confrontation.

Jesus did not heal the blind man or raise Lazarus from the dead merely to make them live comfortably. He was paying a price for the world and His followers had to pay a price, too.

Our service to the poor fails to produce a following often because it is funded from abroad and therefore it does not ask the beneficiaries to pay a price. When Jesus sent the twelve apostles to preach and heal in Israel, He prohibited them from taking money with them (Matt. 10:5–10). The beneficiaries of their healing ministry had to pay for their upkeep and thus become participants if not the owners of His movement. Jesus accepted His death, the price which He paid as a criminal, as His glory, and He carefully chose the time and manner of His own death so that His cause could receive the maximum benefit from His crucifixion.

The purpose of cultivating a mass following was not to gain a selfish crown. Satan had offered the kingship to Jesus at the very beginning of His ministry (Matt. 4:8–10). But He refused to have the kingdom for Himself. He wanted the kingdom for the poor (Matt. 5:3; Luke 6:20), the sorrowful (Matt. 5:4), the meek (Matt. 5:5). The poorer masses saw Him as their Messiah and began to follow Him, which naturally threatened the existing leadership. The Jewish authorities had perceived: 'The whole world is following Him; therefore He has to be eliminated.' The crucifixion, not international recognition, was His real glory, laying down His life for the poor of His nation, the harassed and helpless sheep.

Jesus's service gave Him a mass following which in turn gave Him power. This seriously threatened the Establishment and meant death, which was the final proof of whether Jesus was really serving others or only Himself. An all-out love for God and for one's neighbours has to be tested. Jesus was prepared to be tested by fire.

When people are so committed to changing the unjust social structures in favour of the enslaved, exploited and oppressed that they will lay down their lives for the cause, they are bound to create ripples in history that never cease.

Neither the Jews nor the Romans killed Jesus in order to make Him a sin-offering. The historical cause of His death was that He was a serious troublemaker as far as the Establishment was concerned. Their charge against Him was that He had claimed to be the legitimate king of the Jews, which meant that their rule was illegitimate.

Yet this is not to say that the theological meaning of the cross, that Jesus died for man's sin, is false, less true or historically untrue.

As Jesus hung upon the cross of Calvary, it was literally the sin of the world that was hanging there at that moment of history. The people who physically saw that crucifixion, whether or not they were Christ's followers, saw that it was not the justice but the injustice of man that was being carried out that day. In the arrest, trial and crucifixion of Christ, man's sin was more than visible: man's disobedience to God, man's rejection of truth, man's cruelty, his lies, his hate, his greed, his vested interest, his oppression, his exploitation, his abuse of power, his deliberate choice of evil were all there on the cross for everyone to see, hear and feel. That is why the Biblical statement, that Jesus became the sin of the world, is not some theological mumbo-jumbo, but a statement of historical fact. It was not Jesus who was judged on that cross, but the sin of mankind that was judged and condemned.

The eye-witnesses, such as the dying thief, could see that man's evil was hanging on Jesus's cross. That is why the Bible declares that God has now decreed, that since Jesus loved sinners so much and became the sin of the world Himself on the cross, man can find forgiveness for his sin through faith in the death of Christ, as the final and complete sin-offering. But conversely, if a man does not personally accept the death of Christ as a means to his salvation from sin, then he cannot be saved; he will himself have to take the full consequences of sin before a perfectly Holy God. Many people find it hard to accept that the sacrifice of Jesus on the cross is the only means of finding forgiveness for one's sin. But who else ever became sin for the world? In the whole of human history Jesus is the only one who took man's sin upon Himself.

The Jews did not crucify Jesus to make Him a sin-offering for the world, but since He did become sin on the cross by His own choice, God declared that 'there is no other name under heaven given to men by which we must be saved' (Acts 4:12). Indeed, the New Testament focuses on the theological meaning of the cross, i.e., Jesus as the Saviour from sin, far more than it focuses on the historical meaning of the cross, i.e., Jesus the troublemaker. One of the reasons for this is that the historical meaning of the cross was obvious to the contemporaries of the New Testament writers, whereas the theological meaning needed exposition, defence and practical application. We can ignore the theological meaning of the cross only at eternal cost to ourselves.

However, the contemporary assumption that the historical meaning of the cross is irrelevant, is equally mistaken. Jesus not only carried His cross, but He asked His disciples to carry their own crosses, too. One cannot be a disciple of Christ unless one takes up one's cross and follows Him (Luke 9:23).

What does it mean to carry one's cross?

The capital punishment of crucifixion was the weapon used to perpetuate Rome's reign of terror. Those condemned to die had to carry their own crosses to a public place where they were crucified. Jesus asked His disciples to fight Rome with its own weapon, instead of trying to fight it with the sword.

Mahatma Gandhi well understood and imitated Christ on this point. Some Indians wanted to fight British colonialism with guns and bombs. But Gandhi asked his followers to fill the British jails and accept the British stick-blows and bullets. When the British threw Gandhi in jail, it was not Gandhi who was judged and condemned but the British themselves. When they beat and killed the peaceful protesters, they in fact destroyed their own kingdom. That was what Jesus invited His disciples to do. To 'take up your cross' means to become a rebel, to fight a corrupt establishment with its own weapons, to be a troublemaker and take the consequences of that.

Historically, the cross was the strategy of Christ and His followers in their battle against the powers, principalities and rulers of a dark age. During the day the Jews could not arrest Jesus in Jerusalem, in that week of festivity, because the crowds revered Him as a prophet. They could not arrest Him at night secretly, because He didn't spend the nights in Jerusalem. There was no way they could have arrested Him in the Garden of Gethsemane, even with the help of Judas, because the darkness was to His advantage. A group of soldiers with torches, searching for a man in the woods, face an impossible task. He can slip out in any direction. In our districts of Madhya Pradesh, bandits have dodged whole battalions of police for as many as thirty years in the jungles. Jesus said that no one takes His life from Him (they couldn't), but that He lays it down Himself. Under His Father's guidance, He chose to die, at a time which best suited His purposes or strategy.

On His cross, the Scripture says, He made a mockery of powers and authorities by disarming them, i.e., by making their weapon – the cross – redundant (Col. 2:15).

Today, in many countries of the world where evil, corruption and tyranny reign, heaping untold miseries on the weak and the poor, Christ calls His disciples to a practical compassion for the sheep. He calls His followers to take up their cross and follow Him in the path of service, protest and confrontation.

A man whose perception of Christianity is conditioned by the contemporary image of the Church is very likely to dismiss my interpretation of the historical meaning of the cross as a heresy. But Gamaliel, a respected Jewish rabbi, who watched Jesus and His cross-bearing community closely and sympathetically, saw them as well-intentioned political rebels. He naturally classed the apostles with Theudas and Judas the Galilean who 'also' led revolts against Rome. The entire Jewish Sanhedrin –

both critics and sympathisers of the apostles – agreed with Gamaliel's perception of the Church as a band of rebels (Acts 5:33– 40).

Through His service Jesus deliberately became a champion of the masses. But this does not mean that He went after cheap popularity with the masses. He demanded costly discipleship. Only by creating disciples who are prepared to care for the sheep at the cost of their own lives, can we hope to stand up against the gates of Hades. The Lord Jesus created a mass following, a power base, to disrupt the structures that had kept the blind man a beggar.

Our service today lacks power because it is often marked by self-love, or it is produced by compassion which does not understand the social roots of human misery and gives no answer to them. When we choose to live for others in such a way that we are willing to lay down our lives for them, we shall produce fruit for God, because we shall have power. This will bring honour to God and to us, though through the cross.

A Story from Indian Church History

Indian society has experienced enormous change and improvement during the last 200 years. Many people forget that this process of social change was initiated by Christian missionaries who understood that Christian compassion called for a crusade against those social institutions and practices which oppress and dehumanise man.

The battles against sati (burning of widows), untouchability, child marriage, female infanticide, bonded agricultural labour, drunkenness and opium addiction, were often initiated and led by missionaries. Hindu reformers took up the battle following the missionaries. However, we must admit with shame that when reform began to touch the evil of colonialism itself, the Church backed out, leaving the leadership in non-Christian hands. Nevertheless, there is much we can learn from the early missionaries. One good example was a missionary crusade against the exploitation of forced labourers by the indigo planters in Bengal.

Indigo is a plant from which dye is made. After indigo plantations ceased to be very profitable in the West Indies and America, many European planters came to Bengal and joined the Indian landlords in the indigo plantations. They leased or bought large estates which were rented to Indian peasants for cultivation. Peasants were given initial loans which landed them and their children in virtual slavery. According to the terms of the loan and cultivation rights, they had to grow a fixed quantity of indigo for their landlords' factories, whether or not they could grow any food for themselves.

For decades, when the cost of other agricultural produce doubled or tripled, the price of indigo was kept fixed. The result was that production cost was often higher than the selling price. This kept the peasants on the point of perpetual starvation. If anyone protested, he was kidnapped, locked in a factory and beaten up by the muscle-men of the landlords. The police and judiciary were bought off by bribes. Any honest officers and magistrates could do little because no peasant dared to witness against a landlord or his muscle-men. It was a reign of terror.

These cruel European landlords were a great help to the missionaries whenever they went on their preaching excursions among the peasants. But when the missionaries heard the peasants' tales of woe, they realised that these men with empty bellies could not possibly pay attention to the Gospel. Even if they could hear it, they could not accept it, because the missionaries were patronised by their oppressors, the landlords.

The Rev. F. Schurr, a CMS missionary, was among those who were deeply grieved by the cruelties of the indigo planters. Like Moses long ago, he chose to reject the patronage of the planters in order to participate in the

sufferings of the peasants. He exposed the cruelties of
the indigo plantation system by reading a paper 'On the
influence of the system of indigo planting in the spread of
Christianity' in September 1855 at a conference of Bengal
missionaries held in Calcutta.

This sparked off a controversy. Some missionaries in-
itially opposed the idea of getting involved, but gradually
as the facts became known most joined the battle. The
Hindu intelligentsia and the secular press played helpful
roles. A powerful appeal was made to the Government to
appoint a commission of inquiry and change the system of
forced labour. The planters predictably fought back, blam-
ing the missionaries for leaving religious matters and
meddling in political and secular affairs and creating class
conflict. The Government sided with the planters and
turned down the appeal for a commission of inquiry
without even giving a reason.

The missionaries were infuriated and moved the matter
in the British parliament and aroused public opinion in
Britain and in Bengal. Among the means used were art
and drama. The Rev. James Long, another CMS missionary, translated, published and distributed a Bengal
drama, *Mirror of Indigo*, which was a satire on the indigo
system, portraying the effects of the system on a labourer's
family.

A criminal case for libel was started against him for this
and he was finally imprisoned for serving the oppressed.

Here was a service that stirred up a society, exposed and
condemned the cruelty of a blind Establishment and
brought the cross, power and honour to Christian servants. An Australian historian, G. A. Oddie, wrote thus
about the results of Long's imprisonment:

Long's apparent willingness to suffer for the sake of others
and in the cause of peace with justice for the ryots [peasants]
of lower Bengal, his lack of bitterness and self-regard and his
cheerful acceptance of what he believed was an inescapable
duty made a profound impression. Indeed, his attitude and

stand on the indigo issue probably did more to commend his
faith than any amount of preaching could ever have accomplished and at least for the time being affected Hindu and
other non-Christian perceptions of Christianity. It reinforced
the impression created by the missionaries' earlier participation in the indigo controversy that they totally rejected the
racial arrogance of fellow Europeans and were not 'partakers
of other men's sins'. 'The Rev. J. Long,' wrote the editor of the
Indian *Mirror*, 'has acted manfully and precisely in the manner a true Christian missionary should have done when
placed under the same circumstances.' Dr Kay of the S.P.G.,
who visited Long in prison, remarked on the tone of vernacu-
lar newspapers and quoted one as saying that, if this be
Christianity, then we wish Christianity would spread all over
the country. Duff, Wylie, Stuart and others believed that
Long's imprisonment was creating a very favourable impression for Christian missions and catechists informed
Long, that as a result of his imprisonment, 'people have
listened . . . more willingly to their preaching'.*

It will no doubt be argued that Long lived in British India
and thus was able to speak boldly against 'his own system'.
Modern missionaries in India are prohibited from such
interference. It may be true that as guests they do not have
the right to interfere with our socio-economic system.
But the problem comes when the missionaries (and even
Indian church leaders) prohibit the Indian Christians
from involvement in such daring acts of compassion. They
keep the Indian Church away from the mainstream of
national life, and prevent us from cultivating a feeling
that this is 'our system' and we have not only the right but
a responsibility to love it and make it just.

By the end of the nineteenth century, Jesus had become
the central issue in India, primarily because the missionaries not only evangelised but also led the action for
social reform and upliftment of the down-trodden. J. N.

---

*G. A. Oddie, *Social Protest in India: British Protestant Missionaries and Social
Reforms 1850–1900*, Manohar Publications, New Delhi, 1979, p. 192.

Farquhar, in his classic study, *Modern Religious Movements in India*, published at the beginning of this century, shows that Christ was then the central factor in the ferment in Indian consciousness. All the movements were either responding to Him or reacting to Him.

However, when Indian leadership began to feel that the greatest social evil in India was colonialism, the Church generally withdrew from the arena. Therefore the initiative and leadership of the reform movement passed out of Christian hands. In the 1920s and '30s Jesus became a side issue in India. Missionary statesmen such as E. Stanley Jones realised what great damage a short-sighted Christian leadership was doing to the cause of Christ by not participating in the national struggle for independence. Stanley Jones, therefore, vigorously supported the independence movement. The British Government retaliated by banning his entry into India for five years.

It was most unfortunate that at that time the Indian Church neither stood up for independence, nor even for Dr Stanley Jones who had served the Church as few others did. The result of this non-involvement was that by the 1940s and '50s Jesus became a non-issue in India, Christianity appeared to be a tool of Western imperialism, and Christians began to be perceived as those whose loyalties did not lie with India. This popular misconception continues to make evangelism ineffective. If Jesus continues to remain a non-issue much longer, we shall certainly wipe out the tremendous legacy of the 200 years of missionary service in India.

Take the issue of freedom for women to develop as full human beings. A century ago, when Christians first started admitting girls to school in our district, the Hindu pundits said, 'You might as well educate the cows.' Pandita Ramabai, a brilliant high-caste woman, who founded the Ramabai Mukti Mission (Mukti means liberation), was converted to Christ because she saw Jesus as the true liberator of women (e.g., His dealing with the Samaritan woman in John 4).

Today, Jesus is no longer seen as a liberator of women, even though the evils of female foeticide, female infanticide, child marriage, dowry, bride-burning, forced prostitution, 'flesh trade' (or selling of women as slaves), continue unabated. As the Christian influence declines in India, even the most horrifying ritual of sati has been revived. It was banned 158 years ago primarily due to the efforts of the first British missionary in India, William Carey, who was supported by the British reformer William Wilberforce and the Indian reformer Raja Ram Mohan Roy.

In such a situation where evils continue to be institutionalised, Jesus could be brought back into the centre of the debate by compassionate Christian interaction with the mainstream. Why are we uninvolved? For some it is a matter of lack of compassion – religious service has become a means of self-aggrandisement. For others, it is a theological problem. The action for social reform, they feel, would take them away from their calling to be witnesses. We shall take up this latter problem in the next chapter.

2

EVANGELISM AND SOCIAL REFORM: ALL THINGS NEW

A society cannot be reformed unless it is first informed of what is wrong with it, what is right and how to get it put right. Some societies permit action for reform. They are called 'open' societies. They grant freedom to the citizens to oppose the evil of the rulers. These societies have inbuilt self-correcting mechanisms. But this is a relatively recent phenomenon in world history. Most societies even today are 'closed'. Insiders can hardly speak against the evils in their society, let alone do anything about them. Attacking social evils in these societies is virtually impossible; even preaching takes enormous courage. When centres of power have been taken over by corrupt vested interests, a reform movement has to awaken and organise the common man. In other words, to bring about a fundamental change in the evil institutions of a society, one needs to build up a mass movement. Preaching is the prerequisite for building up a movement, and this can be undertaken by an individual.

In a closed society, preaching is often the only tool available to the reformers. For example, Jeremiah was given the task of reform. God said to him, 'See, today I appoint you over nations and kingdoms to uproot and tear down, to destroy and overthrow, to build and to plant' (1:10). What was Jeremiah's tool for reform? Nothing but preaching. God said to him, 'You must go to everyone I send you to and say whatever I command you. Do not be afraid of them . . .' (7–8).

The fact that a person is only preaching does not

necessarily mean that he is not a reformer. John the
Baptist was a lone voice preaching a new kingdom. But he
triggered off a movement. By the time of Paul, the full-
time preachers of the Kingdom were numbered in scores.
Ultimately, it is ideas, not armies, that rule the world.

Social reform is usually a people's movement which
seeks to remove the evils of society and transform its
unjust oppressive values, ideals, practices and institutions into being just, humane and conducive to human
fulfilment. A movement for social reform is based on:

(a) A critical awareness in a society that their values and
    institutions are fundamentally wrong.
(b) A hope that a change is possible.
(c) A faith that a better alternative is in fact available.
(d) A leadership that is able to organise and mobilise the
    masses against the evil status quo.

Piecemeal social reform is possible. A group of people
may see one particular social evil, protest against it and
set right the injustice. But from a Christian point of view
evil is cosmic, it has a supernatural dimension. The conflict of good and evil is a conflict of two kingdoms – the
kingdom of Satan versus the Kingdom of God. Therefore
an evangelist aims at holistic, not piecemeal, reform. As
St Paul put it, evangelism means 'the new has come' (2
Cor. 5:17). The evangelist seeks to bring the kingdom of
Satan under the righteous reign of God, even though he
recognises that until Christ returns all change is temporary, that the forces of evil will fight back and seek to
corrupt the hearts and institutions of man.

Kingdom of Satan

Some years ago a non-Christian young man was sent to
our community in ACRA. Though he was an intelligent
and pleasant person, he had some deep personality dis-

order which we could not understand. He had been taken to the best medical and psychiatric experts in India, but that had been of no help. After he had been with us for several months some of us began to suspect, for a variety of reasons, that perhaps his problem was demonic. So we began to pray for him. One night as I was riding my motor-cycle back from the town to our village, I felt in my spirit that it was going to be a crucial night for that young man. Soon I found myself praying out loud and singing as I rode. It was past nine o'clock on that wintry night when he met me at the gate and announced that he was leaving us. I requested him to wait till the morning and proceeded to call the community together for prayer. We prayed for him the whole night, but apparently to no effect. He disappeared the next day. We had a great sense of failure and I felt that we had simply made fools of ourselves.*

But there were three young people in our community who did not give up. They began to pray that God would bring a simple case of demon possession before us and initiate us into the realm of the supernatural reality. These three decided to fast and pray over a weekend. On the first night of their prayers, one 10-year-old Hindu girl in our community had an attack of fits, which she had never had before. Her parents decided not to disturb any of us at night, so they didn't tell us. But by the morning she was better, so no one took much notice of the episode.

Two days later she had another severe attack of fits. As I was walking back to my home after morning prayers, I saw her lying on her string cot. She was writhing with pain. She had high fever and in a rhythmic fashion she was lifting her head and banging it back on the cot in much agony.

One of the three young people who had been praying suggested to me that we ought to pray for her as she had an

---

* Months later we discovered that the personality disorder did in fact begin after the boy's uncle had some sorcerers cast spells on him to enable the uncle to take over his father's restaurant business.

evil spirit. The young man's mother, however, insisted that the girl simply had an attack of fits and should be taken to a doctor. I was indecisive, hesitant to say that my Christian friend was mistaken, yet unwilling to make a fool of myself as before when the whole night of prayer ended in failure. I thought it best to have my breakfast before deciding whether to take her to the hospital or to pray.

While I ate breakfast one of our Hindu friends took his bicycle, went to the village and brought back a sorcerer. This sorcerer saw the girl and straightaway abused the demon in filthy language, asking it to come out. To everyone's amazement the girl became normal in an instant.

Naturally I felt humiliated. I had to admit that even though I was a Christian, my secular education had really made me quite naturalistic. Deep down in my mind I was not really sure that evil spirits affected human beings. My Hindu neighbours understood the supernatural nature of the universe much better than I did and were therefore able to handle such a situation more confidently. Our community had another prayer-meeting repenting of our unbelief, praying for another opportunity to discover the power of God.

A week later a 20-year-old man had a similar attack of fits, except that it was much worse. By the time we reached him, he was screaming out loud that he was going to die. He complained of a splitting headache and body ache. He, too, was lifting and banging his head on his bed in a rhythm. We felt that it was the same evil spirit which had earlier troubled that girl. So, we began to pray. We prayed for over an hour but nothing happened. Gradually people began to leave the room. The boy's condition became worse. There was a self-confessed agnostic in the community, who began to mock us as well as advise us to take the boy to the hospital instead of playing with his life.

Finally, only two of us were left praying. Doubts began to come to my own mind. There was nothing much left to pray about, anyway. So I had to choose again; do we take him to the hospital or pray more? With my eyes open, looking at the agony of our friend, I made my decision out loud. 'This time I refuse to be deceived. This is demonic and the evil spirit must go.' At that moment, in an instant, the fever, pain and fits all vanished. The boy got up as if from a trance. He walked with us to the next house where many of the community members were having coffee, and announced, 'I was dying; these people prayed for me and the Lord Jesus has healed me.'

Most Christians, I suppose, will have little difficulty believing that evil supernatural forces exist and bring suffering upon individuals. But in today's cultural climate many may have difficulty in believing that the evil supernatural forces also affect and seek to control the socio-political systems under which we live. The Bible says: 'The devil led Him [Jesus] up to a high place and showed Him in an instant all the kingdoms of the world. And he said to Him, "I will give you all their authority and splendour, for it has been given to me, and I can give it to anyone I want to. So if you worship me, it will all be yours"' (Luke 4: 5–7).

The devil was not bluffing Jesus. Jesus Himself acknowledged that Satan was the 'prince of this world' (John 16:11). St Paul called him 'ruler of the kingdom of the air, the spirit who is now at work in those who are disobedient' (Eph. 2:2).

St John says, 'we know that . . . the whole world is under the control of the evil one' (1 John 5:19).

It was Daniel in the Old Testament who was first given the insight that behind the socio-political evils lie supernatural powers. In Daniel, chapter 2, King Nebuchadnezzar saw the statue of precious metals that represented the four successive empires of gold (Babylonian), silver (Medes and Persians), bronze (Greek) and iron (Roman) and finally a mere stone (the Kingdom of God) which conquered the kingdoms of this world.

In chapter 7, as Daniel, the governor, sought to understand where history was going and God's role in it, he was given the vision of these same four kingdoms – not as the

dazzling statue of precious metals but in their essence and
spiritual nature – as beasts that devour: the lion (Babylonian), the bear (Medes and Persians), the leopard
(Greek) and the 'fourth beast – terrifying and frightening
and very powerful. It had large iron teeth; it crushed and
devoured its victims and trampled underfoot whatever
was left' (Dan. 7:7). This was the Roman Empire. In
contrast to these beastly kingdoms which came out of the
Mediterranean Sea, Daniel saw the humaneness of the
coming Kingdom of God as 'a son of man, coming with the
clouds' (Dan. 7:13). As Daniel fasted and prayed to understand history further, it was revealed to him that the
kingdoms of this world were beastly because there were
evil, supernatural forces behind them. The angel said to
Daniel:

> Since the first day that you set your mind to gain understand-
> ing and humble yourself before your God, your words were
> heard, and I have come in response to them. But the prince of
> the Persian kingdom resisted me twenty-one days. Then
> Michael, one of the chief princes, came to help me, because I
> was detained there with the king of Persia ... Soon I will
> return to fight against the prince of Persia, and when I go, the
> prince of Greece will come (Dan. 10:12–20).

I understood the Biblical teaching that the socio-political
evils have supernatural dimension when I saw the Hindi
film *Ardh Satya* (Half-Truth). It is a film about a police
inspector in Bombay who seeks to fight political/
bureaucratic corruption. The film says that courage and
integrity are half-truths. When a man of great courage
and integrity stands up against social evils, he destroys
not the evil but himself. The film realistically shows that
evil in our social system is far stronger than a heroic police
officer, a journalist, a social scientist, an agitator for the
civil rights movement, or a trade union leader. They can
do little about evil, because they don't even understand its
true nature or power. The film says that we live in a

system where evil is greater than good and it rules. That is what I believe the New Testament implies by the teaching that Satan has taken over the control of this world's kingdoms. Without this perspective, it is impossible to understand adequately how political authority can degenerate to the levels of cruelty and wickedness that it so often does.

The kingdom of Satan begins in the mind. It began when Eve doubted God and believed Satan (Gen. 3:1–6). St Paul also teaches the same truth in Romans 1:18–32. The kingdom of Satan begins when we turn away from truth to believe falsehood. When the mind is darkened, our behaviour quickly becomes immoral. Sin then begins to rule in our bodies. When most people in a society turn away from truth, then that society confuses right with wrong and wrong with right. After affecting our mind and behaviour, Satan then affects the social institutions which our darkened minds build and govern. The human institutions so affected become corrupt, wicked and oppressive. It was the authority and splendour of the oppressive political institutions of man that Satan claimed were his kingdom.

Because of our individualistic outlook modern Christians seem to think that Satan's objective is to lead individual souls astray. But the Book of Revelation reveals that Satan is out to 'deceive the nations' (Rev. 20:3, 8). He 'leads the whole world astray' (Rev.12:9).

What is Satan's basic deception? Again, Revelation says that the plan of the great dragon is to control the political power. The 'dragon [Satan] gave the beast [emperor] his power and his throne and great authority . . . Men worshipped the dragon because he had given authority to the beast, and they also worshipped the beast' (Rev. 13:2–4). It is the 'beast' (the human king – Rev.17:11) who makes war against Christ and wants to be worshipped as God.

The modern secular ideologies which deny God, end up making the state to be the Lord and Saviour. They violate the first of the Ten Commandments, 'You will have no other god besides me', and by making the state 'absolute' and independent of God they turn state into oppressive beast, causing poverty, slavery and war.

'The Truth Will Set You Free'

The rule of Satan begins in our minds, when we choose to believe his deception, and culminates in the oppressive political institutions we build. This means that untruth is the foundation of slavery. Proclamation of truth, therefore, is the basic means of setting people free from oppression and exploitation. Jesus said, 'Then you will know the truth, and the truth will set you free' (John 8:32).

Often we fail to see that the oppressive and exploitative social structures survive not because of the strength of their institutions or their physical force, but by the spreading of their faith. People believe the falsehood, therefore they allow themselves to be exploited.

I grew up in the city of Allahabad in the state of Uttar Pradesh in India. Millions of devout Hindus come there from all over India to bathe in the River Ganges. They know that the Pandas (priests) will loot them. They do their best to protect their money from the Pandas. But they usually return home with stories about the way they were cheated. Later, they return to the Ganges and generally get looted again. Yet they continue coming. Why? Because they believe that the holy waters of the Ganges will wash away their sins and give salvation to the souls of their deceased relatives. Slavery is a matter of belief.

Christians at the time of Martin Luther knew that the Papacy had become an exploitative Establishment, yet they sustained it. Why? Because they were made to believe that the Pope, as successor of St Peter, held the keys to salvation.

'Justification by faith' is the heart of contemporary evangelistic preaching. It was also the heart of sixteenth-century Reformation theology. Then the doctrine of 'justification by faith' created titanic socio-political reforms. Today it creates no ripples. Why?

Then, Martin Luther had courageously added a significant word to the Biblical teaching on salvation by faith, which gave this truth a cutting edge in the then contemporary society. It was the word 'alone'. 'Justification by faith alone' consciously implied that the selling of indulgences by the Pope for the salvation of the living and the dead was nothing but economic exploitation of the masses by a corrupt religio-political Establishment. This doctrine meant that the seven sacraments of the Church were, in the final analysis, irrelevant for salvation. Therefore, the entire army of priests, bishops, and even the Pope, which saw its role chiefly as sacramental, was an unnecessary economic burden.

'Salvation by faith' and 'the priesthood of all believers' were radical truths, not pious doctrines. These truths demanded that the Pope and the entire priestly hierarchy should be opposed because they had sucked Italy economically dry and were now threatening to rob Germany of its wealth.

Luther's preaching of justification by faith alone stirred up the masses because it offered spiritual as well as economic freedom. The masses are rarely moved by theological debates. It was not the theological truth which stirred up the masses. It was the politico-economic implications of the truth, perceived by the ordinary people to be beneficial to them, which generated the mass movement for acceptance of the truth.

Evangelism in the sixteenth century attracted crowds because it freed nations from the yoke of oppression; because it was 'good news to the poor' (Luke 4:18).

Paul's evangelism was exactly the same. Paul said to the Corinthians that when he visited them, he was determined to preach nothing 'except Christ and Him crucified' (1 Cor. 2:2). He preached nothing except Christology and soteriology, i.e. the doctrines of Christ and salvation through the cross. Therefore, we need to look at these two doctrines of Paul to understand how his evangelism set people free from the slavery of oppressive Jewish and Roman systems.

Paul's Doctrine of Salvation

Paul's preaching of salvation through Christ's death on the cross is summed up in two major themes in his epistles – grace versus law and faith versus works.

Paul preached, taught and debated that man cannot be saved by works of the law but by faith in the grace of Christ. Paul taught that by faith in the atoning death of Christ, man can find forgiveness from sin and reconciliation with God. This, according to Paul, meant that there was no further need for circumcision, animal sacrifices, observance of Jewish rituals or special days. Under the law, man had to spend much money to earn salvation; now it was available freely. Believers no longer needed to live under the yoke of the law. This simple but revolutionary message undercut, in one fine stroke, the entire edifice of the exploitative Jewish structure.

Jesus said that he had come to set the captives free (Luke 4:18). Paul was showing how that was accomplished through Christ's death.

The Jews who went to the temple in Jerusalem to offer sacrifices knew that it was a 'den of robbers' (Matt. 21:13). Yet they came, patronised the temple and allowed themselves to be exploited by a corrupt Establishment. Why? Because they believed that they could be saved only through observance of the law.

Declaring that man cannot be saved by the law, but only by faith in the sacrifice of Christ, Paul was destroying the very foundations of the exploitative Establishment. The Jews were naturally threatened by this preaching and as we shall later see they persecuted Paul because of the threat his message was to their whole system.

Paul learnt the basics of his theology from Stephen, who

taught that the temple in Jerusalem was not the heavenly reality it was made out to be by the Jews. Stephen said that God gave Moses the vision of the heavenly reality. Moses made its shadow in the form of a mobile tabernacle. After Israel settled down, David wanted to build a temple. But because David was a man of war God allowed only his son Solomon to build it; which implies that the temple is not the ultimate sacred institution of meeting with God. In any case, God made it plain even in the Old Testament that He, who created the heaven and earth, does not dwell in temples built by human hands (see Acts 6 and 7). This was a message which undercut the whole Jewish system and predictably brought about violent retaliation.

Paul, after his conversion, preached Stephen's message with greater clarity and depth. The message that the work of Christ had made the Jewish law redundant was best summed up by the author of the Epistle to the Hebrews. He said, 'By calling this covenant "new", He [God] has made the first one obsolete; and what is obsolete and ageing will soon disappear' (Heb. 8:13).

Paul was an evangelist because he preached salvation by grace. And his preaching was seen as 'Good News' because it freed his audience from their slavery to the law. When the Jewish converts sought to bring the law back into the Church, Paul fought them, arguing that if that happens, grace will be futile and Christians will be back in slavery. It was Paul's determined fight which finally made the Jerusalem council declare that the law was a yoke on the necks of the disciples which neither they nor their fathers were able to bear (Acts 15:10). Paul's preaching of salvation was thus a message of social reform, of freedom from a yoke.

The late Dr Bhimrao Ambedkar, the greatest leader of the untouchables in India, understood this basic technique of social reform which Paul used. That is why he preached 'conversion' as the answer to the social evil of casteism. It is unfortunately true that Buddhism, to which he led his disciples, has turned out to be a blind alley, but it remains true that a society can be reformed in one of three ways:

(a) One can accept the basic structure of the society, e.g. the Hindu caste system, and seek to minimise injustices inherent in it by law, as the government of India has tried to do for the past three and a half decades. But Ambedkar, who wrote much of India's constitution, knew that this approach could not transform the situation fundamentally.

(b) Therefore, a second option is to refuse to accept the basic structure of an unjust society and seek to change the people on top who are responsible for injustices. It is almost impossible to change the people on top merely by preaching, because they are usually happy with the status quo. As Jesus said, it's easier for a camel to go through the eye of a needle than for a beneficiary of the kingdom of Satan to enter the Kingdom of God. The oppressive, exploitative system is favourable to the people on top, therefore they don't want change.

So, one is tempted to use either violent or non-violent force to overthrow the oppressors. It is possible to overthrow the government by seizing or killing a few or a few hundred people. But what can one do if the oppressors number literally hundreds of thousands, or if they are too powerful to be overthrown by force?

(c) The third option then is to change the oppressed. One can refuse to accept the basic unjust structure of society and reform the system by changing the oppressed, e.g. if the untouchables cannot change the high-caste oppressors, their only option is to change themselves. This change has to be at two levels. First, they have to be set free from mental or ideological slavery. They have to cease to believe that they are born untouchables because of the *karma* (actions) of their past lives and that blessings of their future lives depend on their fulfilling the duties of their present low status. They are held in slavery by faith in a falsehood. The truth alone can set them free from this mentality of slavery. Second, they have to opt out of the socio-religious system, i.e. cease to be Hindus, in order to cease to be untouchables. They have to accept a new world view which has a high view of man and equality of man as basic doctrines and at the same time they have to join a community which practises these truths.

Oppressive systems survive by propagating falsehood. Evangelism liberates by spreading truth, i.e. by undercutting the intellectual foundations of an exploitative system and by creating an alternative social structure which seeks to live out the truth.

Paul's Doctrine of Christ

For Paul, 'preaching the Good News', and 'preaching Christ', were synonymous. Christ was Paul's 'Good News'. Much of Paul's theology is therefore Christology. Paul's Gospel is that 'Jesus is Christ' (or Messiah). The crucified, risen, exalted and soon-returning Christ is the heart of his message. Paul preached that Jesus, who was humiliated on the cross, has now been exalted over all rulers, powers, authorities and dominions of this age as well as of the age to come. This same Jesus, who is going to return soon to set up His Kingdom will destroy the man of sin – the evil ruler who sets himself above God. Paul's Christology was thus a political Gospel. Jesus was presented as King of kings and Lord of lords. Jesus, not Caesar, was the One before whom every knee would bow and whom every tongue would confess to be the Lord.

In his Christology, Paul was not comparing or contrasting Christ with the deities of the then prevalent religious sects. Jesus was the alternative to the emperor and the religio-political ideology of the day. The Gospel was formulated against the background of the imperial faith as the answer to the exploitative empire. Jesus was not another or more powerful god but the only God. He, according to Paul, was the Ruler, the final Authority, the Judge, the King – the Lord.

In a society where the 'dragon' has deceived people into worshipping the beast, Caesar is lord, and 'statism' is the official creed. When the state is the ultimate, the final reality, the absolute or the lord, it becomes the exploiter, the source of most social evils and oppression. In such a setting, preaching of a Lord who as a shepherd or saviour is above the state is exciting news. As Canon Michael Green said,

> If Jesus was going to return as the triumphant son of man in clouds of heaven . . . then clearly here was the final winding-up of history for which they were all waiting; here was the break-in of the theocracy and the defeat of the impious Romans. This must have been a factor in the immediate growth of Christianity from its cradle in Jerusalem.*

It is true that many preachers of Christology teach the divinity of Jesus and His saviourhood, but fail to preach His kingship. Most Christians therefore understand how 'Jesus saves' is good news, but fail to see how 'Jesus is Lord' is also good news. But the wise men who came looking for the baby Jesus in Jerusalem were looking for a king and not specifically for a saviour. Why? Because they were disillusioned with the kings and beastly kingdoms of this world. What were the kingdoms of this world? Brutal! Immediately after the visit of the wise men, King Herod ordered the massacre of boys under two, in and around Bethlehem! There was nothing their parents could do to protect the life of their infants. In such a milieu the news that the Messiah, a new king, is born was indeed good news.

In the Roman world of the first century the message that

---

*Michael Green, *Evangelism in the Early Church*, Highland Books, 1984.

'the kingdom of heaven is at hand' received such a massive response in spite of brutal opposition from the state, because it was presented to a people who believed the prophet Daniel, who had taught that at the time of the fourth empire (after Babylonian, Persian and Greek) the God of Heaven will raise up His Kingdom. The New Testament evangelism meant that the vision of Nebuchadnezzar that during the era of the kingdom of iron, a stone uncut with human hands will smash and destroy the dazzling statue of precious metals (or human kingdoms) and itself become a mighty mountain, was about to be fulfilled.

The original New Testament readers were living in the fourth empire, in the oppressive kingdom of beast, in the darkness of despair and death. The message that the Kingdom of Heaven has come, that Jesus is Christ, naturally stirred up hope and excitement – as well as determined opposition.

Just as Paul's preaching of salvation as a free gift of God, by faith in the cross of Christ, undercut Jewish theology and set people free from the yoke of slavery to the Jewish Establishment, his preaching of Jesus as Lord undercut the theology of Roman imperialism and destroyed political totalitarianism. The common man's excitement at the realisation that Jesus was King was most visible on the first Palm Sunday, when He entered Jerusalem on a colt with a crowd following Him and shouting 'Blessed is the King of Israel' (John 12:12).

The Jews persecuted Paul for destroying their entire system through his preaching of the cross (Acts 21:28). The Romans persecuted him for destroying their imperialism by his preaching of Jesus as Lord. For example, in Thessalonica when Paul preached, 'This Jesus I am proclaiming to you is the Christ' (Acts 17:3), his opponents understood him as 'defying Caesar's decrees, saying that there is another king, one called Jesus' (v.7). Did they misunderstand Paul? If it was a matter of misunderstanding a spiritual king as a political threat, then Paul and the other apostles could have easily corrected that misunderstanding. In fact they would have avoided preaching Jesus as 'Christ' and concentrated on preaching Him only as the Saviour. But they did not compromise their preaching. They knew Jesus as 'the ruler of the kings of the earth' (Rev. 1:5), therefore they preached Him as such. They in fact believed that Christians would rule over the nations of the earth (Rev. 2:26–7). It was natural that such preaching would result in persecution.

We Wrestle 'Not Against Flesh and Blood'

Some Christians may find it hard to accept this insight into Paul's Christology. Paul himself said, they might argue, that 'our struggle is not against flesh and blood' (Eph. 6:12). How can Paul then be concerned with political reform?

Paul did say our struggle is not against flesh and blood, but added in the same verse that we struggle 'against the rulers, against authorities, against the powers of this dark world and against the spiritual forces of evil in the heavenly realms'. Paul did wrestle with evil spirits – the spiritual forces of evil in the heavenly realms. But much of his time was spent in struggling against the rulers and authorities of *this dark world*, who were humans. It was not the evil spirits who beheaded John the Baptist, crucified Jesus, stoned Stephen or persecuted Paul. The Church was and is pitched against the rulers and authorities of this dark world – against those in positions of power and authority, who prefer darkness over light. However, it is also true that there are spiritual forces of evil over these human rulers.

I can understand why Christians living in 'open' societies fail to understand Paul's oblique language of 'powers and principalities'. But they ought to understand that Paul was not living in an open society with freedom of speech guaranteed. In fact, when he wrote the letter to the

Ephesians he was under arrest with perhaps a Roman guard reading what he wrote or listening to what he dictated. How could he say openly that he was wrestling against the totalitarianism of Caesar?

Recently, in one of our villages, a high-caste man beat an untouchable man to death. He ordered his body to be cremated that night, before the police could come or a post-mortem could be done. The untouchables were terrorised. As they have to live in that village they could not oppose the wicked village chief openly. They have only whispered against the 'rulers of this dark world', in a (oblique) language very similar to Paul's.

Evangelism and Political Freedom

Evangelists did not conceive of political freedom in negative terms of the overthrow of the Jewish and Roman Establishments. They understood and preached political freedom primarily in terms of submission of human kings to the rule of God. This is significant because history has not been able to throw up a better understanding of political freedom than this.

There are many nations even today whose understanding of political freedom is no more than skin-deep. Not in a metaphorical sense, but literally. For an average Indian, for example, political freedom is when the white colonial rulers leave and brown, black or yellow natives take over the rule. Most often this colour-of-skin definition of political freedom means worse oppression and tyranny. One does not need to prove the emptiness of this definition. In almost any nation that has attained 'political freedom' since the Second World War, the new rulers are happy with their freedom, but the ruled are usually more oppressed and exploited than before. Colour-of-skin definition of political freedom generally means freedom for the new governors, not necessarily the governed.

Only where the freedom is understood as the rule of law

is there some freedom for the governed. A people are free only to the degree to which the powers of their government are limited by law. There is only one test of political freedom: Are the rulers under the law or above the law? If any of the human rulers are above the law, then that is rule of rulers, not the rule of law. Potentially that is a dictatorship, not a free country. Rule of the human rulers is not freedom. Rule of law is. This raises the fundamental question: What is the source of law – human or divine? If the law is merely human, then those who have the power to make the law have the power to change it, too, and thus they are above the law. Genuine freedom is impossible in societies which have only human law.

Only if law comes from beyond man, can it be binding on all men. Only before a transcendent law can there be a genuine equality of all men. Kings and prisoners alike can be equal before the law if the law itself is above the king. Transcendent law presupposes a transcendent law-giver. If there is no just ruler above the kings of the earth, if He has not given His law to men, then political freedom or rule of law is a sheer illusion, a mirage that is impossible to attain. Man is condemned for ever to live under the rule of 'might is right', whether the might be of a few or of the majority. The concept of the rule of law becomes a super-stition without faith in a just ruler above the human rulers.

Proclaiming Jesus as 'The ruler of the kings of the earth' was, and is, the only genuine way of establishing politi-cally free societies. In this sense evangelism does not overthrow the existing political kingdoms, but by bringing kings under a transcendental law it curtails the arbitrary freedom of the kings and thereby increases the political freedom of the ruled.

Political freedom is determined not primarily by whether or not the king himself is Christian, but by whether or not he is under the law of God. Political freedom will increase in proportion to the submission of the rulers to the transcendent law in their public lives.

Was Paul fighting a corrupt political establishment? No, if fighting is understood militarily, but yes, if it is understood evangelistically. He was witnessing uncompromisingly that Jesus, not Caesar, is Lord. Christ had chosen Paul, precisely for such political evangelism. God said to Ananias, 'This man is my chosen instrument to carry my name before the Gentiles and their kings . . .' (Acts 9:15). Evangelism for Paul was socio-political reform, because it brought the kings of this world under the rule of Christ. Bringing totalitarian human rulers under the authority of a transcendent law, is the highest definition of political freedom that history has seen.

The New Testament teaching regarding the Second Coming of Christ and the Final Judgment of man reinforces the perspective outlined above. The doctrine of the Final Judgment of man affirms the great significance and responsibility of each individual. What each individual does with his or her life is important to God. But this doctrine also establishes the equality of every man, whether high or low, before the law of God. Paul says to the slave-owners that they should treat their slaves in the light of the fact that both they and the slaves have a common master 'in heaven, and there is no favouritism with him' (Eph. 6:9).

The same applies to the human rulers and the ruled, judges and accused prisoners. There is an ultimate equality of all men before the law of God. That is a radical Christian basis for political freedom now on this earth. When an evangelist tells the kings of this earth that they, too, have a king and judge over them, before whom they are as much accountable as any other man, the evangelist curtails the totalitarian powers of the human rulers and demands that they be just. That is what political reform or freedom ultimately means.

From this perspective, doctrines of the Second Coming and the Final Judgment do not give us the right to assume that the world will go from bad to worse, making reform impossible. On the contrary, these doctrines demand that our evangelism should result in curtailing the oppressive totalitarian powers of the human rulers. The kings, presidents and prime ministers of the earth should be brought under the rule of Christ. That is evangelism, and that is also political freedom – curtailing and limiting the power of the State over the individual, demanding that the laws of the State be just in the light of the justice and righteousness of God.

Evangelism frees the powerless individual. It limits the power of government by making Christ the Ruler of the kings of the earth.

We shall return to the subject of evangelism and social reform in the second half of the next chapter. But before I am misunderstood as over-emphasising the social dimension of evangelism at the expense of its appeal to individuals to repent and believe, let us consider the relationship of sin to social evils and salvation to social reform.

3

SIN, SALVATION AND SOCIAL REFORM: A NEW MAN IN CHRIST

The previous chapter sought to highlight some of the social implications of evangelism. That, however, must not undermine the fact that in the New Testament the predominant focus of the Good News is on an individual's salvation from sin. Though in some societies today, selfish individualism is denying people the personal fulfilment which comes from deep interpersonal relationships, one basic evil of our times is to sacrifice the individual for all sorts of supposedly 'social' goods. The 'collectivisation' programmes of the Communist regimes that suppress individuality are too blatant an instance of this evil to need mentioning. But the Communists are not the only guilty ones. The killing of unborn or new-born babies for controlling the population of a nation or the 'happiness' of a nuclear family; the burning alive of a widow (sati) for protecting the property and harmony of a 'joint family'; throwing out peasants from their lands (without adequate compensation) to build dams, are all instances of an evil outlook that forcefully sacrifices the individual for so-called 'collective' good.

The Gospel of Jesus Christ in contrast, offers salvation to every individual. The individual bears the image of God, therefore he is the central object of God's love and salvation. It is the individual who is called to repent of his sin and by faith accept God's offer of forgiveness and salvation.

Social evils are the consequences of the rule of Satan. Satan has authority over us because when we choose to

sin, we choose to obey him. We are individually responsible for our sins. Therefore, salvation from sin is the heart
of a holistic reform.

Let us take poverty as an example of social evils, to see
in some detail how sin leads to the misery of poverty and
salvation to *shalom*, i.e., peace with prosperity.

Sin is disobedience of God's law (or obedience of Satan's
deception). If for our purposes we look only at the Ten
Commandments as part of God's law for us, we can see how
every one of those commands has a bearing on poverty and
prosperity.

1. False Gods

While God was leading the Israelites out of the slavery of
Egypt to the promised land, under the leadership of Moses,
He spoke to His people on Mount Sinai:

> *I am the Lord your God, who brought you out of Egypt, out of
> the land of slavery. You shall have no other gods before me*
> (Exod. 20:2–3).

In this very first Commandment, God reveals Himself as a
saviour from slavery; as one who delivered His people
from oppression and wants to lead them into a land
flowing with milk and honey. He is a personal and moral
being – a God of justice and righteousness. He commands
us not to turn to false gods. This is not so much because
God is somehow hungry for our worship, but because when
we turn to amoral or immoral gods, we soon lose our
freedoms and find ourselves under oppressive systems.

We have already noted in the previous chapter, and
elsewhere I have considered in detail, the fact that submission to false deities results in poverty. The kingdom of
Satan begins when we turn from the true God to false gods.
The personal, moral God is the ultimate truth of the

universe, the starting-point and the reference point of the meaning of everything else.

The failure to know the personal God means that we cannot define the human person either, and as a society we gradually and inevitably sink so deeply into darkness and sin, that our lack of appreciation of personhood leads to institutionalising even murder. William Carey, the first British missionary to India, once saw a basket hanging from a tree. In it lay the body of an infant, half-eaten by white ants and birds. He was shocked to learn that it was a common practice for parents to starve their unwanted infants to death in this way. The fact that infanticide had been given socio-religious sanction was totally intolerable to him. Every year in a festival, parents used to throw their unwanted infants in the 'holy' River Ganges. Carey, therefore, fought to uphold the dignity and value of human life by getting this 'religious' ritual banned in the eighteenth century.

Is twentieth-century man any more civilised, more developed? Not really, except in the sense that he now has the technology to kill as many as 60 million unwanted children every year before they are born. In some ways 'developed' humans are worse. When you do not acknowledge God as Creator, in whose image man is made, you are forced to define man with reference to an ape or simply as a complex collection of molecules. No rational basis remains for treating humans differently from animals or machines.

A society which does not know the Saviour God ultimately loses objective yardsticks for distinguishing between justice and slavery, oppression and development. How is it, that in spite of the immense advance in knowledge and power, so many governments in the twentieth century have been able to justify large-scale oppression in the name of development or social engineering, and describe slavery as 'revolutionary freedom' of the left or the right?

It really should not surprise us because the aim of the

'old dragon' is to make nations worship the 'beast' – the emperors that oppress. Communism is the clearest example of the folly of modern man who turns away from the Saviour God to put his faith in a party or a dictator. But Communism is by no means the only such folly. Western secularism also ends up at the same point, denying God and deifying the state. It hardly matters whether we have a leftist saviour or a rightist saviour. Any deity other than *the* Saviour, God, will lead us to bondage and poverty.

2. Worship of Creation

God commands:

> *You shall not make for yourself an idol in the form of anything in heaven above or on the earth beneath or in the waters below. You shall not bow down to them or worship them; for I, the Lord your God, am a jealous God, punishing the children for the sin of the fathers to the third and fourth generations of those who hate me, but showing love to a thousand generations who love me and keep my commandments* (Exod. 20:4–6).

Some years ago I was invited to a village where some poor people wanted us to start development projects. When I reached there, they had just finished cremating a dead body and were making an offering to demons. My friends proudly showed me their temple in the middle of the river, which they said was a thousand years old.

I said to them, 'Do you know why you are poor? It is because your forefathers feared and worshipped the river instead of harnessing its water for your fields.'

Today that village has some believers as well as a government-constructed lift-irrigation system, which has transformed their agriculture (though the high-caste men have begun to grab by fraud and force those previously unproductive lands, which the untouchables have made productive).

When we worship creation we become incapable of exercising dominion over it. A society which worships the cow, becomes incapable of manipulating or improving its breed. A tribe which worships the 'mountain god', instead of looking under the mountain for, say, copper, is doomed to poverty. The tragic consequences of these sins last for generations.

Faith in a personal Creator sets the philosophical framework for faith in an objective, rational creation, whose laws are both discoverable as well as harnessable by human rationality because man is made in the image of a personal God. Societies which substitute faith in a personal Creator for faith in chance or impersonal energy or consciousness, eventually lose a concept of rational creation altogether and are forced by their own logic to deify the forces of nature as well as to consider the objective world as somehow unreal, merely a projection of consciousness.

The eleventh-century Hindu philosopher Shankaracharya, for example, has been the most influential thinker of India. He taught strict monism called *Advaita Vedanta*. According to him, the diversity or plurality of the world is Maya (illusion) or dream of Brahma (Universal Consciousness), who is the only reality that exists.

Prior to this teaching, India made significant advances in science, mathematics, astronomy, architecture, arts, grammar etc. But after Shankara, there was stagnation and deterioration.

This monistic philosophy had two damaging, albeit logical, implications for India.

First, rationality was rejected in favour of mysticism. Our rational consciousness, including our self-consciousness (sense of individuality) was logically seen as illusory. Rationality was considered to be the source of our ignorance or bondage, which makes us see ourselves as distinct individuals instead of God. Meditation, yoga, Tantra, etc., became proper epistemological means to transcend the bondage of rational consciousness and find

reality (Brahma) in mystical experience. The denial of
rationality in favour of mysticism meant that science
became impossible.

Second, because reality was thought to be one, it was
logical to assume that nothing else existed except God.
Therefore the worship of stone, snake or sex was worship
of God. No wonder that after Shankaracharya Indian
society degenerated into superstition, sorcery and a host of
social evils.

The stream of Western thinking which gave up faith in
the infinite personal Creator is now being forced by the
logic of its unbelief to give up faith in a rational creation,
too. This is clearly seen in contemporary science fiction
movies that grapple with the concept of time and stretch
the Einsteinian concept of space–time continuum to imply
that time is illusory. The film *Star Trek IV*, for example,
explores a reality where the twentieth and twenty-third
centuries exist simultaneously. A person can travel from
one to the other in an instant, providing he has the
technology to go fast enough.

Such a view of time could provide no rational basis for
development, i.e., alleviation of human misery or even
ecology with which *Star Trek IV* is concerned. This view
would ultimately mean that not only time but creation
itself is illusory. If the twenty-third century already exists, why save the whales for it as the heroes of the film
do? What significance can human action have if history
is not moving, if we go 'back to the future'? What significance does man or his work have if time and history
are not real?

The pre-Einsteinian rationalists who conceived of time
as 'absolute' were wrong. Because God alone is absolute,
time and especially our perception of it cannot be absolute.
We perceive everything from a relative standpoint
through various media. When we see a coin, for example,
in a bucket of water, the coin is not where it appears to be,
because water has refracted the rays coming back from the
coin. However, the fact that our normal perception of the

coin is inaccurate, does not make the reality of the coin
itself illusory. Time is not absolute but it is real.

God created for six days and rested on the seventh; this
means that what came to be on the second day* was
non-existent on the first. Man and creation are also real.
But they are not to be worshipped. God made man from the
earth. Therefore man is a part of creation. But God
breathed His spirit in man and therefore he is different
from the rest of creation. He bears the image of the
Creator. He is creative. He is to be a worker in God's
creation, exercising dominion over it, not worshipping it.

Recently, the Prime Minister of India spoke to the
United Nations' General Assembly against the Western
tendency to have 'dominion over creation'. He advocated
the view that man should seek harmony with nature, not
authority over it. In his own country, however, he would
like to assume authority over people and would have
everyone believe that his exercise of authority is not only
good for people but also necessary. And that is true of
course. If men who have greater intelligence than any
other creature, need human authority over them, would
not the non-rational things and forces of nature require
greater exercise of intelligent authority over them for
order and development?

The Bible says that people who worship dead wood,
metal or stones eventually become dead in their minds,
too. Those who worship demons become demonic to the
point of sacrificing their own children to appease their
deities.

Another reason why we should not make images of God
is because God has made His image Himself – man. Man is
made in the image of God and therefore He is the one to be
respected and served, not the idols made by human hands
and imagination. That is sin.

---

*I am not implying that six days necessarily mean six 24-hour periods. What a
day means on earth is not what it means on Venus or Jupiter. Genesis specifies
that by one day is meant one evening and morning – not 12 or 24 hours.

3. Lack of the Fear of God

You shall not misuse the name of the Lord your God, for the Lord will not hold anyone guiltless who misuses His name (Exod. 20:7).

Gods of stone, wood or metals do not save. But the living God does. He made man in His own image that man may have fellowship with Him and serve Him. Man has turned away from Him and consequently gone into slavery. But God still takes the initiative to rescue man and to enter into a covenant relationship with him. Even though we have sinned and joined the dark side, He is willing to be our God, our Father. He is willing for us to use His name, to have all the privileges and power that come from His name. But unlike other gods and goddesses, He is not a power that men can manipulate for their advantages through magic, sorcery, rituals, offerings or sacrifices. His name is not a mantra (sacred sound with occult power) like that of the demons, to be chanted for occultic power of mystical experiences. He is a person. He is a Holy God – a judge. Therefore, He is to be respected, worshipped and obeyed.

The proverb says that 'the fear of God is the beginning of wisdom'.

A mind which fears God stays away from evil and loves truth and righteousness. Because it fears God, it ceases to fear man or the kingdoms of man. It also ceases to fear nature, but sees it as a mission field.

The first Commandment to have no gods other than the Saviour God deals with the state of our minds – whether we believe in truth or falsehood. The second and third Commandments which prohibit the worship of creation and exhort us to revere the living God, deal with the attitudes that result from our beliefs. It is not enough to believe in the Saviour God. We must revere Him.

Not taking the name of the Lord in vain implies a deep commitment to walk in integrity, with a sense of personal responsibility for our thoughts, words and actions. The truth is that we are morally responsible creatures, therefore accountable to God. This fact demands that we should build our lives on the foundations of the fear of God.

Can a business enterprise succeed where the workers have no respect for those in authority over them? Can the larger human endeavour to find *shalom* – peace with prosperity – succeed without a fear of God born of a sense of human accountability to Him? For a finite creature living in God's universe it is sheer foolishness and arrogance to disregard and disrespect God. It will not go unpunished. The greatest of human minds are no more than those of little boys playing with pebbles at the shore of the sea of knowledge. Just as an astronaut is certain to destroy himself and his spaceship unless he obeys the instructions of others who are better informed than he, man destroys himself without humility, meekness and reverence towards the infinite, personal God, the Saviour God who has allowed us to use His name. This commandment means that He saved Israel from slavery; He is leading them to prosperity; but He is a Holy God, not to be taken for granted or used for our vested interests.

4. Neglect of the Sabbath

Remember the Sabbath day by keeping it holy. Six days you shall labour and do all your work, but the seventh day is a Sabbath to the Lord your God. On it you shall not do any work, neither you, nor your son or daughter, nor your manservant or maidservant, nor your animals, nor the alien within your gates (Exod. 20:8–10).

This fourth Commandment deals with the necessity to work for six days and to rest on the seventh day. Some people sin by not working diligently for six days, whereas others, driven by greed, unbelief or other circumstances do not rest on the seventh day. Either way of breaking this command results in poverty. The necessity of work flows out of man's special position in the world as God's vice-regent, implied in the first three Commandments. It is not enough, not to worship creation. God put Adam in the Garden to 'till it and keep it', therefore human fulfilment comes from work. Not to work is sin.

A person who makes no distinction between creation and the Creator first begins to worship creation. Then he interprets creation as somehow unreal, and therefore a life of work as a life of bondage. His goal or salvation then becomes to go into an ashram (a-shram or non-labour), away from a life of action to a life of meditation.

As the Western mind increasingly moves away from the Christian world view it also appears to be moving away from faith in work to a faith in meditation, magic, occultism, spiritism, yoga, etc., as means of acquiring power over creation. Even cult movies such as the *Star Wars* or *Star Trek* series reflect this, often showing magic to be greater and more desirable than the powers of science and technology. This represents a gradual move of a culture from truth to deception, from responsible freedom to the slavery to superstitions and demons. We in India know the result of this intellectual suicide. This Commandment warns against it.

A life of meditation, when it means a negation of work, is a life of suppression of human creativity or a denial of the image of God in man. It does not require academic expertise to know that a culture which does not put a premium on work comes under the grip of poverty. 'He who works his land will have abundant food, but the one who chases fantasies will have his fill of poverty' (Prov. 28:19).

P. T. Baur, of the London School of Economics, has challenged the consensus of the economists who think that the prosperity of a nation depends on its climate and natural resources. He did his pioneering studies in the rubber industry of South-East Asia in the 1940s and '50s and found that the Indians harvested half the rubber that the Chinese did when they were working on the same plantations. From this he learnt that it is not physical resources but human values and attitudes that make the critical difference between prosperity and poverty.

In my own experience of the rural life, I learnt that one important cause of poverty was that the high-caste Hindus worked only when forced to by necessity, otherwise they generally considered work to be degrading.

The work ethic of the Indians working for their Government is a handy subject for the cartoonists. But it is sad that so many of the educated youth in Third World countries bribe to get a Government job precisely because they believe that it means secured salary, perks and 'extra income' without much exertion.

The command to work for six days and to rest on the seventh implies that even though the Saviour God has delivered Israel from slavery in Egypt and is taking them to a promised land – 'a land flowing with milk and honey' (Deut. 26 and 27) – yet economic prosperity will not be there lying around to be picked up and enjoyed. No, His people will have to work for it.

Yet work eventually ceases to be meaningful and fulfilling unless it is seen as a part of the overall purpose of human life in relation to both creation as well as the Creator. If work is to be a vocation, a 'call' transcending drudgery, then it has to be seasoned with Sabbath rest. The Sabbath is not merely a physical and mental rejuvenation. It is holy. It is meant to service our hearts and minds with the divine perspective on life. Therefore, it is primarily a spiritual rejuvenation. It is the spirit which must govern our minds and bodies. Whether work is the never-ending drudgery of a housewife washing dishes and mopping floors or a watchman staying awake night after night, or a strenuous effort of an astronaut in space for months, the Lord's Sabbath can give meaning and inspiration to make their labour not only tolerable but also a work of art pleasing and satisfying. By keeping the 'Sabbath to the Lord your God' you bring your life and work under God. The work then becomes a 'call'. It inspires the worker to persevere, to work for a cause higher than mere bread and butter.

St Paul says that a man who does not work but steals as his means of livelihood, must begin to work after he comes to Christ, not merely to be able to eat, but so that he can create enough wealth to be able to give to those who are in need (Eph. 4:28).

To disobey this command is to sin with far-reaching socio-economic consequences.

5. Dishonour for Parents

Honour your father and your mother, so that you may live long in the land (Exod. 20:12).

Man cannot exercise authority over creation, without being himself subject to authority. Only those who honour authority over them, can handle the power of authority over others.

The family and parental authority are the sources of respect and obedience for authority, and wisdom comes from age and experience. Honouring parents is the necessary preparation for a life of useful work, which is taught in the first four Commandments. To dishonour parents or other authorities is sin: it leads to a chaos of conflicts and unhappiness. Respect and obedience for authority lead to order, peace, fruitfulness and life.

This fifth command to honour parents underlines the importance of family life. In some societies individualism is destroying the family. In others, collectivism often destroys the family as the primary educational and economic unit. Both individualism and collectivisation are, therefore, sinful.

Israel was a patriarchal, tribal society. The 'family' was not merely a social unit, but a civic, economic, military and political entity, too. So this command implies not

simply that we honour our fathers and mothers but that
we be law-abiding citizens, respecting authority.

We have seen in the previous chapter that an assumption underlying the preaching of the Kingdom of God was
that the Roman empire was the fourth beast of Daniel 7:7
or the empire of iron of Daniel which was smashed to
pieces by the stone of the Kingdom of God (Dan. 2:34,
44–5). St Paul learnt from his own experience, however,
that the grace of God was not absent even from wicked,
totalitarian kingdoms. The Jews would have killed Paul,
had it not been for the Roman law which held that an
accused had a right to defend himself before a judge as well
as to make an appeal to higher authorities, up to the
supreme court of Caesar himself. Therefore Paul taught
Christians living in Rome to pay taxes and respect civic
and political authorities (Rom. 13:1–7). It is only by a life
of consistent obedience that we earn the right to disobey
human authority when that has to be done in order to obey
the higher authority of God.

When family is the business enterprise, it does not
require any imagination to see how to break this Commandment will result in poverty. Can an enterprise be
profitable without respect for and obedience to superiors?

God says we must honour and obey those over us so that
we 'may live long in the land'. One very important cause of
the relative weakness of the economic life of Third World
countries is that family-owned economic enterprises are
suspected, whereas artificial co-operatives, societies or
state-controlled 'public sector' companies are promoted.
More often than not these ventures fail because they do
not do justice to 'human factors' in economic life. In
contrast, Japanese experiment has shown that even large
multinational companies do better if a family spirit is
injected into management.

But the command to 'honour your father and mother' is
not to be obeyed primarily because of its economic benefits. In fact it is sinful to respect only those who have
economic or intellectual power. Children may well have

more knowledge or money than their parents, but that
does not justify disrespect for poor or illiterate parents. If
parents are to love and care for powerless, illiterate infants then when children grow up, they should reciprocate
respect and care for parents who may by then have become
powerless. A society which does not care for parents will
soon lose the rationale for caring for children too. God says
that if you wish to live long in the promised land, you must
honour your father and mother. And we should note that
mother is to be respected and obeyed as much as father.

Old-age pensions, retirement benefits and other forms
of social securities for the aged are to be welcomed as
positive developments. But when these become substi-
tutes for the love and care of the children for their parents,
then these measures, instead of being expressions of the
respect for the parents, become an expression of the selfish
individualism of a society which is bound to be as destructive of the family as collectivism. The promise of *shalom* –
that you may live long in the land – is dependent on the
continuity of right relationships in the family.

6. Murder

The Commandment '*You shall not murder*' (Exod. 20:13)
implies that man has a God-given right to life of which he
cannot unjustly be deprived. God is pro-life. Jesus said he
came to give life abundant, whereas the one who gives
death is a robber. Man as the creator of wealth is more
important than land, cattle, capital or machine. It is not
enough to respect only God or parents. We must respect
all of human life, including those under our care and
authority.

One of the earliest lessons I learnt in our development
work in the rural areas of a dacoit (bandit) infested district
was that a chief cause of poverty was the absence of the
security which comes from a stable law and order system;
where to have wealth means to invite robbers, people

prefer either to remain poor or move out of the villages to the more secure context of cities. Those who are able to save a little money in the village choose not to invest it in a rural-based enterprise. The commercial banks are often reluctant to invest in perfectly viable projects in villages, because of lack of security.

A society which cannot put the security of human life as its top priority cannot hope to rise above poverty. Therefore the sixth Commandment not to commit murder, is fundamental for prosperity.

Like all sin, murder begins in our minds, in a lack of a clear understanding of who man is, in a lack of respect for human life. The evolutionary view that far from being sacred, life was a product of blind chance meant that Hitler, who believed in the doctrine of the survival of the fittest, could first order execution of all the terminally sick patients in Germany and then of six million men, women and children, whose only crime was that they were born to Jewish parents. Reverence for life implies that our right to life is not absolute. We do not have a right to suicide. 'My life' is not mine – it is God's gift to me. Besides, I have debts to repay to my family, my society and to my God. So it is important that we develop an attitude of respect and gratitude for life.

In India socio-religious sanction for murder of infants and burning alive of widows became possible without any Hindu guru challenging the evil, because the doctrine of reincarnation of the soul meant that life is not something sacred but a bondage or *sansara*. The goal of Moksha (Salvation) was understood as cessation of our individual existence, i.e., merging of our individuality into Brahma (the Impersonal Consciousness).

Philosophies that imply a low view of human life are to be shunned as evil. But we must recognise that we may hold to the correct doctrine and yet in practice hate our brothers, which, said Jesus, is as bad as murder in God's sight (Matt. 5:21–2).

Today, atheistic secularism justifies taking away

human life by giving it a less objectionable name than murder, such as abortion or euthanasia. Once the doctrine of the sanctity of life has been rejected and a philosophy of death accepted, we have already lost the battle for development. For the secular mind, poverty issues are more important than pro-life issues because it puts the purse above the person. Politicians are always talking about the poor because the poor have votes whereas unborn babies don't.

Jesus, however, says that human life is far more important than economics, i.e. what we shall eat or wear (Matthew 6:25–34). The command not to commit murder defines the boundary of our authority, as well as constantly holding before us the purpose of our salvation and of all our work, i.e., life.

7. Adultery

God says, 'You shall not commit adultery' (Exod. 20:14).

One of my frequent themes in our villages is that the economic bullock cart of India is moving very slowly because it is being pulled only by one bull – the male. The woman is usually confined to the chores of the home. The reason for women's enslavement is rampant sexual immorality. We cannot afford to give freedom to village girls to go to high schools in towns because we don't trust our men to leave them alone. Therefore, they often have to remain uneducated, unskilled and treated as economic liabilities. Even in the West the growing acceptance of the single-parent family almost inevitably means a poor family, and emotionally handicapped children. Very often the system of social security gives financial incentive for claimants to remain single-parent families. This not only impoverishes them but puts a financial strain on society, too, which ultimately cannot but be destructive to moral values, to the institutions of marriage, family and economic life as a whole.

We can give freedom to our women only when we trust our men. Trust is possible only in a society which has a high sexual ethic. A low sexual ethic first results in the breakdown of marriage and then eventually in loss of freedom for women, as a means of protecting the family. Both have far-reaching economic consequences.

In 1980, my wife and I were invited for a lecture tour of Holland. On the first night our hosts put us up in a Christian hostel in the middle of the 'red light' district of Amsterdam. In my lectures that week I often joked with my audience.

'I thought I was coming from an underdeveloped country to a developed society. But on my first night here I learnt that I have come from a culture that is about a thousand years ahead of yours. What you have in Amsterdam now, we had in our "temples" in Khajuraho a millennium ago and we know well where that road leads.'

Young people today often live in tension. On the one hand, there is the tradition that you can depend on your parents for financial needs only as long as you are unmarried. On the other hand, the marriage age is being pushed back because of the need for academic specialisation to get good jobs. More and more people are resorting to premarital sexual relationships. In some countries this seems to be gaining social acceptance.

There can be no doubt that once sex is permitted outside of marriage, there is not much hope of protecting the institutions of marriage and family. The way out of the dilemma should be family support for married children, instead of encouraging them by default to live together before being married.

To break God's law for personal convenience is extremely dangerous and in the long run destructive of stability, peace and prosperity.

During 1975–7 when India went through its brief phase of totalitarianism called 'Emergency', I was amazed to discover that even our population control measure – of forcefully sterilising men – failed in spite of the brutal use

of the state power because of the low sexual ethic in the
countryside. It was the village women who resisted the
programme. The reason was simple – if they became
pregnant after their husbands had had a vasectomy, how
could they 'show their faces to anyone'? They did not think
that it was possible for them to protect themselves from
the lust of the other men around them. Therefore they
could not allow their husbands to go through the vasectomy operation. Thus the sin of adultery became the real
hindrance to the control of a growing population.

8. Theft

The Commandment *'You shall not steal'* (Exod. 20:15)
implies that I have a right to property of which I cannot be
deprived unjustly. Security of life and property create a
context in which economic development can take place. A
society which cannot protect the wealth of its citizens from
thieves or a state which robs its citizens of their wealth
through unjust tax structures or by denying them the
right to property, cannot hope to get out of the clutches of
poverty. On the other hand, if the citizens steal the taxes
which should go to the Government, they impoverish and
weaken their society. Therefore, the command 'You shall
not steal' is another pillar on which a prosperous society
stands. The sin of theft breeds poverty.

The Indian Government is rocked today by scandals
that almost two hundred and fifty thousand million rupees
have been hidden away by Indians in foreign banks as
'black money'. Much of this money has been generated by
the politicians and bureaucrats as illegal bribes on im-
ports and exports. But much of it is also money generated
by legitimate business which is not brought into the
country to evade taxes. The businessmen feel that the
Government will steal their money through unjust tax-
ation. So they prefer to steal taxes from the Government

themselves. We have a joke: When a politician steals public property in the West he goes to jail; when he steals it in India, he goes to the West – preferably to the Swiss banks. Some national leaders feel that the present situation is worse than the British Raj taking away to England the wealth that Indians had created.

One of the ways in which the business community stole the wealth of the ordinary people in Biblical days was through 'unjust weights and measures'. Moses prohibited such theft in his law. The prophets denounced it as sin. But today many economies lower the value of their currency as the simplest way of stealing the wealth of the people – in the name of 'development'. When people ultimately lose faith in Governments' paper money, the country goes through the upheavals of bankruptcy.

This practice of stealing by devaluing currency, which is the modern equivalent of using changeable weights and measures, seriously hinders progress in poor countries. It serves as a disincentive to saving. A person who saves a hundred thousand rupees to enable his child to start a commercial enterprise may find that by the time the child is ready, the value of his savings has gone down to (say) only seventeen thousand rupees. In contrast, a person who had taken a loan of a hundred thousand rupees may find that it was very profitable to have been in debt because the real value of his liability over the years has decreased on its own to only seventeen thousand rupees. It then becomes wiser to have liabilities instead of savings and investment. A society which prefers to have liabilities instead of savings, for fear of the theft of its people's savings by the state, cannot get out of its poverty.

Property rights, like the 'right to life', are not absolute. In the Jubilee legislation, for example, the Lord says, 'The land must not be sold permanently, because the land is mine' (Lev. 25:23). A man who becomes a drunkard or a gambler cannot have the right to sell off his capital assets on the grounds that 'it is my land' any more than he can take his own life on the plea that 'it is my life'. Ultimately the land is not his. It is God's gift to him. He is required to develop it for his children and grandchildren, not fritter it away.

Some interpreters think that Leviticus 25:23 implies that we have no property rights. From God's statement 'the land is mine', they somehow derive a socialism which says 'the land is the state's'. Nothing could be farther from the truth. Jubilee law implies that private ownership is so fundamental that basic capital assets in Israel could not even be sold. This is not a question of taking sides in an academic debate between the right and the left. The future of a whole society depends on whether or not its people have security of property rights. A man is likely to recharge his soil and develop his land best, if he knows that his descendants have to live off that land for generations to come. The family ownership of capital is the best way to preserve and strengthen the eco-system. The ideologies that deny property rights to families destroy their capital. Why would a man plant a tree and nurture it unless he is either paid for it or he has a reasonable basis for thinking that his children and grandchildren will get the timber and fruit from that tree? It is folly to deny property rights to people and then demand that they plant trees or recharge soil. Economic development is built on the foundation of security to property implied in the command, 'Thou shall not steal.'

9. False Witness

You shall not give false testimony against your neighbour (Exod. 20:16).

Personal integrity is fundamental for a just social order. A few years ago a Sikh, who had done business both in India and England for years, taught me the significance of honesty to poverty and prosperity.

He said to me, 'Why don't you settle in England and do business here; it is very easy and much more rewarding.'

I was surprised how a man who could not speak one correct sentence in English could succeed in business in England. So I asked him, 'Why is business easier in England than in India?'

'Because everyone believes you here,' was his reply. As a businessman he knew the relationship of truthful witness to the economic prosperity of a society.

Successful commercial activity is built on trust, which in turn depends on the truthfulness of the people. Where people do not respect their own words, they create conditions of conflict, chaos and suffering. They build a society on the premise of distrust.

In 1980 I walked with a friend in Holland to a dairy farm. There was no one in the sales room. He opened the tap of the milk container and filled his jug. Then he put a banknote in the money bowl lying there, took out the change from the bowl, put it in his pocket and started walking back home.

I was amazed. 'If it were India,' I said, 'you would probably take home both the milk and the money.' But then, in a flash of insight, I saw the relationship of moral integrity to economic prosperity.

'If the farmer had to employ a salesman,' I said, 'our children would get less milk than they do now, because it would be more expensive. In any case, if people are dishonest how can you trust a salesman? We have milkmen in India, but we can never trust that they have not mixed water in the milk.'

In 1983, I was again in Holland, waiting with my daughter for a tram in Amsterdam. I asked two American girls, 'Where can I buy tickets for the public transport system?'

'Why do you want to buy tickets?' they asked, rather surprised, and added, 'We have been going round the town for three days now, and no one has bothered to check whether or not we've bought tickets.'

'You should be grateful,' I said, 'that you still have enough honest people here that the system can cope with a few dishonest ones. If the proportion of the dishonest grew, then they would have to employ inspectors to check your tickets and then the tickets would cost more. Dishonesty would spread to the management and maintenance of these trams, too, and you would have too many break-downs and accidents, and you would wreck a beautiful system.'

In one of our projects we enable peasants to solar dry potatoes into wafers. Then we grind the wafers into potato powder. One peasant farmer whose family has found this to be a very profitable project was pleading with me, 'Why don't you allow me to set up a grinding unit in my own home for making powder?'

I replied, 'If we can set up the powder-making unit in your home we can sell powder cheaper than anyone else in the world, because we shall eliminate packing, transport-ing, warehousing costs of wafers. But the problem is that wheat flour is so much cheaper than potato powder. How can I be sure that you will not mix it in the potato powder to make more money? The costs of dishonesty in India are so high that the Dutch can sell their powder to us much cheaper than we can sell ours in our own country.'

The consequences of dishonesty on economic life are bad enough, but when false witnesses destroy a judicial sys-tem, then a society has to reconcile itself to living in oppression and violence. Principles of justice and civilis-ation then give way to the law of the jungle – 'might is right.' Eventually the judiciary and the State themselves lose all legitimacy because the State becomes most corrupt and oppressive in using the judiciary to pervert justice. Stalin and other Communist dictators made a mockery of justice in eliminating millions of their opponents through sham judicial trials, which were among the darkest epi-sodes of our century. But even in countries like India which have inherited a fair and independent judiciary from the British, the ruling powers are now using the judiciary to protect criminals and harass and punish political opponents through resort to false witness. This cannot but destroy the legitimacy of the State itself.

10. Covetousness

> *You shall not covet your neighbour's house. You shall not covet your neighbour's wife, or his manservant or maidservant, his ox or donkey, or anything that belongs to your neighbour* (Exod. 20:17).

The tenth Commandment takes the earlier nine Commandments from the external sphere – idolatry, murder, theft, adultery, etc., to the inner attitude. Our faith in God's goodness and love for us must result in contentment and thankfulness. Our respect for our neighbours and their property must mean that we work for what we want to and need to have, instead of coveting what our neighbours have. I must create a house I can be proud of instead of coveting my neighbour's. I must work at loving my own wife, to have happiness in my home.

Under the impact of Socialist thinking, many of our leaders in India and in some other Third World countries have told us that we are poor because the Western world is exploiting us. The way out of poverty, therefore, is for us to get their money. All exploitations, of course, must cease – though we must realise that often our own leaders are the greatest exploiters of our countries – but coveting our neighbour's wealth ultimately is an attitude that cannot help. If I have a right to enjoy the wealth I create, so does my neighbour. Exploitation is nothing but the result of covetousness.

Not having a covetous disposition means not only contentment, thankfulness and industriousness – to earn what we want – but also an attitude of loving our neighbour and giving of ourselves to others. We have a right to protect our properties, but it does not mean that we should hoard what we have, irrespective of the needs of others around us. Not being covetous means that we respect and care for our neighbour's rights and needs. This creates the environment of harmony and co-operative action necessary to fulfil our human destiny on earth.

Covetousness is a result of our lack of faith in God and a lack of love for our neighbours. That is why it is a destructive sin.

Sinfulness, Repentance and the Dignity of Man

A reform movement is built on the assumption that man – including the insignificant and enslaved man – is worth fighting for. How does the Christian view that man is a sinner provide the basis for a fight for the dignity of man?

Logically man became human – a creature endowed with free will and moral choice – only when he was given the command, 'Thou shalt not'. The concepts of responsibility and dignity have no meaning without a real choice being given to man. The command gives man the opportunity to exercise his free will. Instead of obeying his instincts alone, he can make real moral choices too. Instead of obeying instructions as a robot, he can choose to obey out of love and gratitude.

It was unfortunate that man exercised the option of choosing to disobey, to sin, to alienate himself from his Creator. The choice to sin meant believing something false and following Satan. By his choice man went from light into darkness. His mind was darkened; his heart was hardened; and his conscience became increasingly insensitive to truth. The spiritual life of man was dead. He ceased to have fellowship with God and he grew to love the darkness of evil. He became a slave to sin, that is, increasing compromise with sin meant decreasing freedom and power to choose what is right (Rom. 7:14–24). As sinner man is guilty – worthy not of respect but of punishment, of eternal separation from God, i.e., hell.

But the Good News is that man is still an object of God's love. God loved man enough to send Jesus to take man's sin upon Himself on the cross. Jesus became sin for us. He took our punishment. He died so that we may find forgiveness and life; so that we may come out of darkness into the joy of God's light. For a sinner, a life of dignity begins in repentance. The view that the human creature has a dignity means that man is a responsible creature. Individuals are personally responsible for sin. To repent is to own responsibility for one's choices.

As slaves of sin we may have forfeited the power to choose what is right, but we have not lost the ability to choose to repent of our sin. A great man is one who shoulders great responsibilities. True greatness therefore must begin by owning responsibility for oneself. For a sinner who has broken God's Commandments to own responsibility means to repent; to ask for forgiveness; to get right with God; to be born again; to get out of the slavery of Satan and begin a life of obedience to God – a life of responsibility to walk in truth, in the light. This is salvation – to find forgiveness and reconciliation with God through repentance and faith. This is also the beginning of a holistic reform.

Ordering our lives conscientiously, or walking moment by moment with a deep sense of personal responsibility within the framework of truth, releases that human initiative, energy and creativity which can generate prosperity and lasting peace.

Salvation and Social Reform

The God who set the Jews free from the slavery of Egypt told them how they could both maintain this freedom and turn it into prosperity.

So be careful to do what the Lord your God has commanded you; do not turn aside to the right or the left. Walk in all the way

that the Lord your God has commanded you, so that you may
live and prosper and prolong your days in the land that you
will possess (Deut. 5:32–3).

Sin breeds poverty. Repentance from sin and obedience of
faith result in *shalom*.

St Paul says that salvation means that a man, who was
dead in transgressions and sins, has died with Christ –
because Christ died for our sins – and has risen with
Christ to newness of life. 'Therefore, if anyone is in Christ,
he is a new creation; the old has gone, the new has come' (2
Cor. 5:17).

The renewal of society begins with renewal of individuals who pass from death to life, from unrighteousness
to righteousness. It is a modern folly to assume that the
key to the economic prosperity of a society depends primarily on its collective programmes, communes or co-
operatives. This misguided belief moves even Christians
to spend their energies in trying to work exclusively for
'community organisation' or 'community development'.
The fact is that very often no entity called 'community'
exists in a given situation. In our villages, for example,
where many Christians and secular groups are working
for 'community development' nothing called community
exists. What exist as social realities are individuals,
families and castes. A reform movement which seeks to go
to the roots, must therefore go to the individuals and
families.

The true key to *shalom* lies with the quality of life the
people lead. It will help us to see the relationship of
salvation to social reform if we see the necessity of relating
justice to righteousness. The Scriptures say that justice
and righteousness are the pillars of God's throne, i.e.
Kingdom. In the kingdom of Satan the two are separated.

Righteousness is the personal dimension of moral law;
justice is its societal expression. More often than not, the
world replaces righteousness with ideology. Then ideology, not rightness of an act, determines whether it is

judged just or unjust. The consequences of this are
terrible.

For example, the Bible says that a dispute should be
settled on the basis of right or wrong (righteousness), and
the judge should show partiality neither to the rich nor to
the poor (Leviticus 19:15). In many countries, such as
India, socialistic ideology says that the law should protect
the interest of the poor. A landlord or landlady is assumed
to be rich and a tenant to be poor. The tenant can stay in
the house and not pay the rent for years, but the landlord
cannot get possession of the house without prolonged,
expensive litigation. The result is that people consider it
foolish to invest their wealth in building houses and
renting them out. They prefer to hide their money in
secret Swiss accounts, away from the sight of the tax
authorities. The poor then have to live in slums or in the
streets because wealth is not being invested in the business of housing – which should normally be a very attrac-
tive business, considering the demand.

Illustrations can be multiplied to show that if justice is
separated from righteousness or God's moral law and
attached to an ideology, then justice becomes oppression
and hurts the poor and the weak whom the 'ideology' was
seeking to serve in the first place. It is like Communist
ideology which claims to be the dictatorship of the proletariat, but ends by denying the proletariat the rights to
organise themselves into unions or even to speak freely in
their 'own' system.

When Jesus asked us first to seek the Kingdom of God
and His righteousness before bread and clothes are added
unto us (Matt. 6:33), he spelt out the necessity of salvation
to *shalom*.

In search of bread the poor are not to follow the revolutionary who takes up the banner of justice rooted in
ideology, even if his argument is that God is biased towards the poor, therefore the state and the law should also
be biased. God is concerned with righteousness. He calls
the poor to repent of their sin, including their sin of faith in

the secularised idols of ideologies. Salvation (or clothing ourselves with righteousness) has to precede *shalom*. Justice must grapple with issues of righteousness (right and wrong) or the personal dimensions of moral law.

Salvation is necessary for social reform because the Kingdom of God is built on righteousness and justice, whereas the kingdom of Satan is often built on ideology and injustice.

In the preceding pages we have seen the roots of social evils in our individual sin and of *shalom* in our righteousness. But it is important to remind ourselves that social reform is dealing with societal issues. An individual may be righteous, freed from the power of sin in his life and yet not be free to be his creative, enterprising self in his own country.

For example, simple hard-working Indians perform economic wonders in Europe or America or even in some Asian and African countries – where they may not even have the elementary political power of a vote. But within India the same people find that they cannot prosper because they do not have the right political connections. The political-economic system has been bent by the powerful to suit their vested interests. In such situations the task of the reformer is to break the chains of oppression, so that the individuals are free to be themselves. Therefore, having reminded ourselves that socio-political freedom is worth something only if the people are free from the power of sin in their individual lives, we should briefly reconsider the significance of the role of an evangelist to the issues of social reform.

An evangelist who seeks to convince people that they are not just living in the kingdom of Satan, but that they are personally responsible for sin, spreads critical awareness. He seeks to inspire people with hope for a better future. He gives them faith that a change for the better is possible. He seeks to bring them out of the kingdom of Satan, into the Kingdom of God – to a state of heart, where individuals will bow before God and refuse to compromise with evil, even if it costs them their lives. Thus the evangelist becomes the forerunner, pioneer or leader of a reform movement.

Paul: An Evangelist

Paul has become a model of an evangelist who holds evangelism to be his priority and sticks to it. Paul claimed that he preached nothing but Christ and Him crucified. He exhorted Timothy to do the work of an evangelist (2 Tim. 4:5). But for Paul, evangelism was a most potent, viable and God-given tool for reform.

Paul's evangelism did not aim at simply renewing people's hearts. Christ, according to Paul, was making all things new (2 Cor. 5:17). Salvation begins in the heart, transforms the mind and is expressed in the behaviour, life-style and relationships of an individual (Rom. 12), who becomes a new man in Christ. But Paul was excited about the great mystery of the Gospel because it was creating a new race (Eph. 2:11–12). Existing religions had become walls that separated Jews and Gentiles. The Gospel was breaking down barriers – the very things which gave social identity to people. The Gospel was creating a new man. That is why Paul's preaching of salvation was seen as a threat to the social status quo and opposed both by Jews and Gentiles.

Paul: A Reformer

Paul was persecuted because he was perceived to be a troublemaker, a man who was turning the status quo upside down by his preaching. The Thessalonian Jews said to the city officials, 'These men [Paul and Silas] who have caused trouble all over the world have now come here' (Acts 17:6). The Jewish lawyer Tertullus accused Paul before King Felix, 'We have found this man to be a

troublemaker, stirring up riots among the Jews all over
the world' (Acts 24:5).

When Paul was arrested in Jerusalem (Acts 21), he was
at the temple. He did not believe in Jewish ritualism, yet
under advice from James and the elders of the Jerusalem
church, he was financing the purification ritual of four
Jewish converts. Paul willingly submitted to what he
believed to be slavery, i.e., economic exploitation in the
name of religion (Gal. 3 and 4), in the larger interest of the
fellowship of believers and in order to earn the right to be
heard within the Jerusalem church.

Paul was not evangelising in Jerusalem, but keeping a
low profile. Yet he was the one who was arrested. James
and the other elders were 'converting' the Jews, but they
were not arrested. Paul who was not witnessing about
Jesus, but observing Jewish rituals, was arrested and the
Jews were anxious to do away with his life. Why?

James, the Jewish converts and other evangelists were
not persecuted because 'all of them are zealous for the law'
(Acts 21:10). They were part of the Jewish sub-culture.
Their message no longer had a cutting edge in their
society.

Paul, however, was arrested, not because he was
preaching the 'simple Gospel' but because the Jews said
that he 'is the man who teaches all men everywhere
against our people and our law and this place [the temple]'
(Acts 21:28).

Jesus had taught that Israel needed to do only two
things for salvation, i.e., repent and believe in Him. The
implication of this is that the Jewish Establishment had
become irrelevant for Israel's salvation. The temple, in
fact, had become 'a den of robbers' (Matt. 21:13), the
Jewish leaders had become a pack of 'wolves' (Matt.
10:16). Jesus had rejected the temple and declared that it
would be so thoroughly destroyed, that not even two
stones would remain joined (Matt. 24:2). The temple, the
heart of the Jewish Establishment, had become the seat of
corruption, exploitation and oppression of the common

man. God, the Father, had vindicated Christ's rejection of
the temple when He made the curtain of the temple split in
two from top to bottom (Matt. 27:51).

Yet, the temple and the Jewish legalism which Jesus
had rejected were gradually creeping back into the life of
the early Church. The Church was becoming culturally
contained within the Jewish status quo. Instead of setting
people free from the slavery of the law and the Jewish
Establishment, their evangelism was beginning to rein-
force their hold. The elders of the Jerusalem church
seemed pleased that the new converts were 'zealous for the
law'. The Church stood in danger of becoming a tool of the
corrupt oppressive Establishment. No wonder it was no
longer persecuted. It wasn't a threat any more. But Paul
was still a troublemaker. He had been insisting that
Christians who were not living out the social implications
of the Gospel were hypocrites (Gal. 2:11–13), carnal
(3:1–3) and cowards (6:12). They were compromising with
the Gospel because they did not want to be persecuted.
Paul insisted that Christians who were compromising
with the surrounding Jewish culture by going back to the
law were not merely backsliders; they were backsliding
away from the grace of Christ into the slavery from which
Christ had set them free (Gal. 5:1–12).

Paul said that he was not persecuted because he
preached the cross (everybody did that) but because he
preached cross only (Gal. 5:11; 1 Cor. 2:2). The 'cross only'
meant that circumcision, law, the temple and sacrifices
were irrelevant. These were religious means of enslaving
people, and slavery was not an abstract concept but social
oppression and economic exploitation. The Gospel, for
Paul, was the power of God for salvation, not only from sin
but from slavery to the law as well. It was a force for
reform.

Therefore, even though Paul asked Timothy to teach the
churches to pray for kings and authorities so that Christians might lead peaceful and quiet lives (1 Tim. 2:2), he
also told him in unqualified terms that 'everyone who

wants to live a godly life in Christ Jesus will be persecuted'
(2 Tim. 3:12). A Christian does not seek to create trouble,
but he does because he is personally and stubbornly committed to live a godly life in a crooked generation. He is
committed to preach truth in a society which is built on
falsehood. If one is to bear witness to truth in such a way
that it will destroy the very foundations of the wickedness
of the society in which he lives – he indeed needs power.
And to that subject we now turn.

4

THE HOLY SPIRIT AND SOCIAL REFORM: YOU SHALL RECEIVE POWER

Just before His ascension Jesus said to His disciples, 'But you will receive power when the Holy Spirit comes on you; and you will be my witnesses . . .' (Acts 1:8). Superhuman power is needed for witness if it means calling not only small individuals but rulers themselves to acknowledge Jesus as Lord, to repent from their evil ways, to reform. God said to the prophet Ezekiel that he was being sent not to a people who would respond to his preaching in great numbers, but to a people who would not listen because they were 'hardened and obstinate'. Therefore, God said, 'I will make your forehead like the hardest stone, harder than flint. Do not be afraid of them' (Ezek. 3:7–9). Jesus's promise of power came in response to the disciples' question, 'Lord, are you at this time going to restore the kingdom to Israel?' (Acts 1:6). Jesus said that their attitude should not be to know the times and merely wait for God to usher in His kingdom. But their job was to go into the world, filled with divine power, and boldly witness to the kingship of Jesus, thereby bringing the world in subjection to the authority and rule of God (see Acts 1:8, Matt. 28:18–20). That is 'evangelism'. That is also the reform of a rebellious and corrupt humanity.

After the disciples were baptised by the holy Spirit, Peter, quoting the prophet Joel, said that the result of the outpouring of the Holy Spirit would be that young men would see visions, old men would dream dreams and all God's men and women would prophesy (Acts 2:17–18).

In the Old Testament, Joel painted that grand picture of what the restoration of Israel would mean. Restoration was not merely deliverance from foreign rulers and an abundance of food, fruit and wine (Joel 2:18–22). It was also an outpouring of God's Spirit and a great outburst of inspired, healthy, positive creativity, manifesting itself in a quality of life and godly culture that brings praise to God (Joel 2:26–9).

In a stagnant, enslaved society, old men do not dream dreams; they mourn for bygone glories. Young men are not inspired by visions of hope for the future; they resign themselves to live with the present static reality of despair and gloom. The creative springs of life dry up, and there is no song of praise in the hearts of slaves. People perish because there is no prophetic vision. No one speaks for justice and truth with the freedom and authority of God. Not only the masses but also the mighty bow before evil and prefer to be discreetly quiet.

Israel had been a stagnant, enslaved society till the day of Pentecost. Individuals like John the Baptist and Jesus had been murdered, but no one had the courage to speak for justice and truth. But the outpouring of the Holy Spirit made the difference between death and life. An ordinary man like Peter became like a mighty prophet of old. With the thundering authority of divine courage, he confronted Israel with its cowardice and cruelty in crucifying Christ. That was powerful prophetic witness to the truth. With the coming of the breath of God the dry bones had come to life and become a mighty army (see Ezek. 37:1–14).

Gift of the Spirit: Prophecy

The New Testament talks of many gifts and the manifold fruit of the Holy Spirit in the lives of believers. We need to look at one gift – prophecy – and one fruit – love, to see how the power of the Holy Spirit is essential for social reform. The New Testament Church considered prophecy as more important than the other gifts of the Holy Spirit, since prophecy is the reforming witness to the truth of God (Rev. 11:3; 19:10).

Today, the terms prophecy and evangelism are often kept strictly distinct. That distinction may have academic value. In real life they are not separate. For example, in 1 Corinthians 14, where Paul exhorts believers to seek the gift of prophecy, he says that if an unbeliever walked into a Christian meeting where everybody was prophesying, 'he will be convinced by all that he is a sinner . . . and the secrets of his heart will be laid bare. So he will fall down and worship God . . .' (vv.24–5). Thus prophesying and evangelising are not two distinct activities. An evangelistic message from God is a prophetic message. In the New Testament sense it is usually called evangelistic rather than prophetic because the emphasis of this message is on evangel or good news of forgiveness rather than judgment as was often the case in Old Testament prophecy.

A prophet is an evangelist because he primarily brings God's promise of forgiveness and salvation instead of judgment. Therefore, when the New Testament asks us to seek the gift of prophecy, it asks us to be evangelists. We are to preach repentance to our generation. Repentance not only for immoral behaviour but also for untrue beliefs. One reason why the Church is so ineffective today is that even though we do speak against personal sin, we choose not to challenge the falsehood which our society believes in. In India we find evangelists preaching against smoking and drinking, but we rarely find someone preaching openly against idolatry. Yet false belief is the foundation of many a human misery, as we have seen in the previous chapter. Because our message rarely touches the miseries of the common man, it does not appear to many to be good news. The Holy Spirit gives us the power for reforming witness because He gives us the gift of prophecy, which includes the power to judge and protest against the evils of the kingdom of Satan.

The Power to Judge and Protest

Proclaiming Jesus as the King of Heaven does not generally result in persecution. But when we start proclaiming Him as the Ruler of the kings of the earth, we invite trouble. Because then we automatically judge the world around us by the yardstick of His justice and righteousness and demand that His will ought to be done on earth, as it is in Heaven.

It takes enormous power and discernment to judge the powers and principalities which are committed to corruption and cruelty. But that is what Peter, empowered by the Holy Spirit, was doing in his sermon on the day of Pentecost. He charged his audience with the sin of cruel murder: '. . . you with the help of wicked men, put Him to death by nailing Him to the cross' (Acts 2:23). And again, 'Therefore let all Israel be assured of this: God has made this Jesus, whom you crucified, both Lord and Christ' (v.36). The Bible records that with many other words, he (Peter) warned them, and he pleaded with them, 'Save yourselves from this corrupt generation' (v.40). That was prophetic evangelism.

Such prophetic evangelism judged a specific sin, which in fact was the extent of blind, naked, unashamed cruelty to which that society had degenerated. Peter also judged the fear, cowardice and the blindness of the masses which allowed corrupt rulers to kill a good, innocent man, whom the people themselves acknowledged as a prophet from God. That fearful cowardice which permitted evil to reign was one of the main causes of the evils in their corrupt society.

Peter's exhortation to 'save yourselves from this corrupt generation' was not merely a message of repentance from private sins. It was a continuation of the theme of the kingdom of Satan versus the Kingdom of God, started by John the Baptist. Proclamation of Jesus as Christ was a proclamation of His kingship; of the beginning of the renewal of Israel; of the start of the Kingdom of God.

The crucifixion of a righteous man was a symptom of the degeneration of a whole society. That symptom was what Peter attacked. In those public statements, made at the risk of his life, Peter was judging the evils of his day, protesting against them publicly and calling for repentance and change. His accusations were so pointed and so directly against the unjust official stand of the state (i.e., Jesus was a criminal) that his hearers had no option but to repent or to kill him. That was prophetic evangelism at its best.

This kind of witness obviously calls for great power and one major aspect of the power of the Holy Spirit is the power to judge the world.

When St Paul said in 1 Corinthians 4:20, 'For the kingdom of God is not a matter of talk but of power,' what did he mean? The context clearly means the power to judge, the power to 'whip' (v.21). Paul confronted the sin of adultery in the Church at Corinth. He said that the Church ought to have the power to judge the adulterer, 'When you are assembled in the name of our Lord Jesus and I am with you in spirit, and the power of our Lord Jesus is present, hand this man over to Satan, so that his sinful nature may be destroyed . . .' (1 Cor. 5:4–5). The Christians at Corinth were taken up by the gifts of the Holy Spirit, especially the gift of tongues. Paul told them that the power of the Kingdom is not manifested by words alone, but in the authority to judge and punish sin.

Christian officers in government and the secular world are often respected for their integrity and ethical standards, but the same cannot always be said about some of the leadership of churches and Christian institutions. And even Church leaders who have personal integrity do not always seem to have the power to judge the sin within the Church. But is this power to be exercised only within the Church? Paul goes on to say in the same context that the saints have to judge the world (1 Cor. 6:2). Are we going to judge the world only after Christ returns?

In the *judicial* sense of the word *judgment* (which carries with it the authority to punish), the saints will judge the world after Jesus returns (1 Cor. 5:9–12; Rev. 2:26–7; 20:4–6). But in the *moral* and *prophetic* sense of the word *judgment*, our task begins when we are empowered by the Holy Spirit. Jesus said, 'When he [the Spirit] comes, He will convict the world of guilt in regard to sin and righteousness and judgment' (John 16:8). How will the Spirit convict the world? Obviously through the Spirit-filled believers.

But if we judge the sin of the world, the world is bound to persecute us. Jesus was not killed because He showed the way to Heaven to man. He said that the world 'hates me because I testify that what it does is evil' (John 7:7). We have to witness or testify not merely about who Jesus is but also about what the world is. The Bible says that we must expose the works of darkness (Eph. 5:11). We need power to do that because when we judge the world, the world retaliates by judging us. Stephen was stoned to death because he said to the Jews in Jerusalem,

> You stiff-necked people, with uncircumcised hearts and ears! You are just like your fathers: You always resist the Holy Spirit. Was there ever a prophet your fathers did not persecute? They even killed those who predicted the coming of the Righteous One. And now you have betrayed and murdered Him (Acts 7:51–2).

That was prophetic witness and it requires power from above. Even the mighty men of this world are usually too weak to stand as witnesses against the evils of their contemporary powers and principalities. They consider compromise to be wisdom.

God's holiness means that He hates evil. His hatred is expressed in two ways – He saves men from sin and He also judges sin. Salvation and judgment are the inseparable sides of the same coin – God's holiness and hatred of evil. The Church as Christ's body is meant to be both an agent of salvation and an agent of His justice. The loss of this balanced perspective has robbed the Church of her dynamism to transform society. Protestantism no longer protests against evil, because it sees itself merely as a channel of God's salvation and not of God's justice. What does it mean for Jesus to be the Ruler of the kings of the earth if He does not judge them? What good is it if His Spirit does not empower those whom He fills to pronounce prophetic judgment?

After His resurrection Jesus said, 'All authority in heaven and on earth has been given to me' (Matt. 28:18). Paul said that the Head of the Church is already seated on the throne above all powers, principalities and rulers of this world (Eph. 1:20–3). This means that Christ's Body has to carry out His instructions and orders. The Church is His mouthpiece. And to be a prophet means to be the mouthpiece of God (Exod. 4:14–16).

This loss of perspective which separates prophecy from evangelism, preaches salvation without proclaiming repentance and justice, reduces the Church to a rudderless boat floating at the mercy of social currents, some of which are ghastly in their cruelty and injustice. Some Church leaders, for example, are enthusiastic to marry homosexuals, but too timid to oppose the annual murder of sixty million babies through abortion. Today we seek the patronage of the Pharaoh in order to preach to the enslaved people. We do not dare to witness to Pharaoh himself.

But the tragedy is that when we cease to be a voice for justice, we also become ineffective as channels of salvation: When we are not breaking the yoke of oppression, we have no 'good news for the poor' either. The poor masses consider us irrelevant and our critics legitimately dismiss us as giving 'opium', and not spreading the Good News.

Martin Luther's preaching on justification by faith alone was a judgment of a Roman Establishment that had become corrupt. That is why it required enormous power, and that is why it resulted in such great reform and many conversions. Paul's preaching of Jesus and His cross, as we saw in Chapter 2, was the judgment of Jewish and Roman exploitative Establishments. That is why he was seen as an opponent of the Jewish law, of the enslaving temple worship and traditions. No wonder Paul needed power from above for such preaching. Such witness has to be stamped with one's blood. It has to be a cross-bearing witness. The tragedy of the contemporary Church is that those Christians who rightly stress the necessity of the work of the Holy Spirit in our lives, are often mistaken about the purpose of God's gift of the Holy Spirit to the Church. They mistake *signs* to be the *reality* itself. They seem to think that the Holy Spirit is given primarily to empower us to do the 'miracles' whereas God said:

> I will put my Spirit on him [my servant]
> and he will bring justice to the nations . . .
> A bruised reed he will not break, and a
> smouldering wick he will not snuff out.
> In faithfulness he will bring forth justice;
> he will not falter or be discouraged till he
> establishes justice on earth . . . (Isa. 42:1–4)

It is a great folly to dismiss this as 'the Old Covenant'. The Lord Jesus Himself said:

> The Spirit of the Lord is on me, because he has anointed me
> . . . to proclaim freedom for the prisoners and recovery of sight
> for the blind, to release the oppressed (Luke 4:18).

Miracles are 'signs' of the Kingdom. Justice and righteousness are its contents (see Ps. 45:6–7).

The Power for Cross-Bearing

Jesus, who commissioned His disciples to go out as His witnesses, called them to a life of cross-bearing. The disciples were willing to drink the cup, the passion and humiliation of the cross, which Jesus drank (Matt.

20:22), but did not have the power to do so. Jesus said that their spirits were willing but the flesh was weak (Matt.26:41).

Jerusalem had crucified Jesus because He claimed to be her legitimate king. For one to reassert in Jerusalem, within two months of Christ's murder, that Christ was indeed the King, was to woo death. How could the disciples, who had earlier fled from persecution, bear witness to Jesus's Kingship without receiving strength which came from beyond themselves? For such a witness, they needed more than the power of oratory, the power of tongues, and the power to perform miracles. The disciples were able to perform miracles long before they were baptised with the Holy Spirit on the day of Pentecost, but they were too weak to face persecution (Matt. 10:1; Luke 10:17). What they needed was the courage to confront their corrupt and cruel society with its sin, call it to repentance and take the consequences of such a confrontation, i.e. persecution.

This was precisely the transformation which the baptism of the Holy Spirit brought about in the disciples. When the Jewish leaders who had killed Jesus and arrested the apostles came face to face with the courage of 'unschooled, ordinary men' like Peter and John, 'they were astonished' (Acts 4:13). The leaders imprisoned, threatened and flogged the apostles, warning them not to speak in the name of Jesus. But the disciples had the strength to disregard the warnings, rejoice in persecution and deliberately choose to disobey the state. That is evangelism.

That is also civil disobedience. By disobeying the state, the disciples affirmed that there was a law and a law-giver higher than the state. They affirmed that the present leadership was unjust, immoral and unworthy of obedience. By their disobedience, they proclaimed that they had a new King; that they were subjects of the Government of God. Their willingness to suffer and die was a testimony to their certain knowledge and faith in the resurrection.

Cross-bearing is the original version of civil disobedience. It is a Christian's submission to the higher law of God, a deliberate rejection of the immoral laws of the state and a joyful acceptance of the consequences of that stand.

Cross-bearing is not easy, and that is why before his arrest in Gethsemane Jesus asked his disciples to 'Watch and pray, so that you will not fall into temptation' (Matt. 26:41). One needs power for cross-bearing witness. That is why Paul prayed for the Colossians that they might be 'strengthened with all power . . . may have great endurance and patience . . . (Col. 1:11). Paul asked Timothy to 'be strong in the grace that is in Christ Jesus . . . endure hardship with us like a good soldier of Jesus Christ' (2 Tim. 2:1–3).

Thus the power for prophetic evangelism is the power to bear courageous witness to the truth and accept persecution from those who are committed to suppress the truth with unrighteousness.

Willingly to choose suffering and self-sacrifice for the sake of righteousness is to walk the way of the cross. It is to engage in a moral and spiritual conflict with the powers and principalities. You stand for truth; they stand for oppression. They stand with the sword. You stand with the cross, the symbol of self-sacrifice. Cross-bearing means power because choosing suffering means fearlessness. The kingdom of Satan is the reign of terror (Heb. 2:14–15). Social evils in the kingdom of Satan continue to exist because people are too afraid to resist them at personal cost. If we oppose the corruption of powers and principalities, we are threatened, harassed, persecuted or ultimately killed. That is how oppressive societies perpetuate their injustice. The cross does not mean accepting injustices. It means refusing to accept what is unjust and taking the consequences of that stand, even if it results in death.

While glancing through the Gospels one sees that Jesus emphatically taught His followers not to fear those who could kill the body. This fearless willingness to suffer is a prerequisite to prophetic evangelism. God said to Jeremiah,

> Stand up and say to them whatever I command you. Do not be terrified by them, or I will terrify you before them. Today I made you a fortified city . . . to stand against the whole land – against the kings of Judah, its officials, its priests and the people of the land. They will fight against you but will not overcome you (Jer. 1:17–19).

> Let goods and kindred go
> This mortal life also
> The body they may kill
> God's truth abideth still
> His kingdom is for ever.

That was the Christ-like attitude of Martin Luther which made the Protestant reformation possible. In our day Lech Walesa, the Nobel Peace Prize winning labour leader of Poland, a Catholic, has exhibited similar power:

> Never shall we make alliance with kings,
> Never shall we bow our necks to might;
> It is from Christ we take our order,
> Each of us Mary's knight!

> We shall not kneel before the power of authority . . .

> Hunger nor misfortune shall break us.
> Nor the world's flattery shall lead us astray:
> For we are all the recruits of Christ,
> Each of us in His pay!*

---

*These are the first and last stanzas of 'The Confederate Song', quoted from Maria Janion's article 'Lech Walesa: A Worker' in *The Other Side*, New Delhi, Nov. 1983.

Fruit of the Spirit: Love

A fearless prophet, defying the state, preaching judgment and repentance, facing persecution, creates the image of a rough and rugged man. But Jesus had asked Peter to take loving care of His tender lambs, to feed and protect them (John 21:15–17). The Kingdom of God was for the meek and the lowly (Matt. 5:3–5).

God in His Kingdom has:

> . . . scattered those who are proud in their inmost thoughts
> He has brought down rulers from their thrones . . .
> but has lifted up the humble.
> He has filled the hungry with good things
> but has sent the rich away empty (Luke 1:51–3).

The disciples, like normal human beings, were looking for great power for themselves in the Kingdom of God (Matt. 18:1–6; 20:20–3). Their favourite topic of debate was, 'Who is the greatest among us?' But the power of the Holy Spirit was not for one's self-glorification; it was for serving others, especially the powerless.

Jesus continuously taught His disciples that to be great they had to humble themselves and become servants. He tried to teach them that the kingdom of Satan was for the big, but the Kingdom of God was for the little children, the nobodys. This verbal teaching was not enough. Jesus also gave them object lessons by blessing the children, by becoming a servant Himself and washing their feet. But teaching and examples were not enough. They needed power to become servants. They needed the power to see that the great dreams of the restoration of Israel had meaning only if the powerless people had a central place in those dreams.

It takes great vision and power to become a servant in a selfish, exploitative society. That is what the baptism of the Holy Spirit achieved in the disciples. Their eyes were opened to see the needs around them and to respond to those human needs with tenderness and the Holy Spirit's resourcefulness. Earlier they had seen the lame man at the beautiful gate as a beggar. Now they saw him with eyes of compassion, as a human being in need of something more than money. Their love for him was the fruit of the Holy Spirit in them (Gal. 5:22). A Christlike compassion and character is what the Holy Spirit produces in those who seek Him. That is the primary work of the Holy Spirit in all believers. By the Spirit's power we first *become* witnesses, then we are able to give credible witness.

The Holy Spirit not only gave the apostles the power to have compassion for the insignificant crippled beggar, He also empowered them to heal the beggar, to meet his need.

We cannot belittle the supernatural gifts of healing, casting out demons and performing miracles. I have seen these miracles take place in answer to my own prayers, as well as those of others who have the gift of healing. But we must remember that the power of performing miracles was not a result of the baptism of the Holy Spirit. The apostles were given that gift much before their experience of Pentecost. What the baptism of the Holy Spirit did for them was to make them servants. Earlier they had exulted in their power to perform miracles (Luke 10:17–20). Now they exalted Christ, as His servants. They not only healed the sick and cast out demons, they also looked after the widows, the orphans, the poor and the drought-stricken (Acts 6:1–4; 4:32–35; 2 Cor. 8,9, etc.).

A prophetic judgment of oppression, cruelty and exploitation in our society can have no meaning if it is not backed by our own life of service and the care of the powerless lambs. But our service also has little effectiveness if it is not seen against the background of our overall Christlike compassion for man. We have seen in Chapter 1 that Christ's compassion was not some sentimental pity or charity. It grew out of a prophetic insight into the social evils of His day. Jesus saw the crowds as harassed and helpless sheep, whose shepherds had turned into wolves. He was moved enough to cry, outraged enough to condemn and concerned enough to identify Himself with them so fully as to lay down His life for them. That is compassionate service. Naturally it calls for supernatural power – the power to deny ourselves, take up our cross and follow the Good Shepherd.

There is no dearth of Christian service today. But because much of it is service without prophetic compassion, it is powerless to bring about a radical change in individuals and society. To be a Good Samaritan has eternal value in itself, but that is not the highest ideal of Christian service. It is only the beginning. A concern for the wounded and robbed man must lead us on to a prophetic judgment of the systems that violate the rights, dignity and values of man made in God's image.

Our service will have a cutting edge when it is seen against the background of our overall concern for man. A prophetic judgment of all that dehumanises man in our society gives meaning and power to our service towards those wounded and crushed by the same society. But in order to be credible, our prophetic words must be backed by service, by a practical affirmation of the value of man. A prophet may stand outside society, but a servant gets inside and dirties his hands. For a prophet to have his message heard, he has to become a prophet-servant.

Such service which grows out of a prophetic compassion brings one power because it makes one a good shepherd. Jesus had compassion for the crowds because the Jewish political, economic, civic and religious leaders, who should have been shepherds to the people, had instead become wolves (Matt. 9:36). The crowds sought Jesus because they were looking for a shepherd, a new leader. Jesus, therefore, sent His disciples to preach, to serve and become shepherds to those lost sheep (Matt. 10:6–8, 16). Jesus's mission was to become the shepherd, to take over leadership from the wolves.

The role of a shepherd, community leader or reformer gives social power. Jesus used that power as a deterrent against His arrest (Luke 20:19). He had been to the temple many times and was no doubt indignant at its corruption. But He did not challenge it until He had a crowd behind Him, shouting His praises. The High Priests and soldiers were afraid to arrest Him for they feared the crowds would take to rioting. John the Baptist had remained a prophet, so it was easy to arrest and kill him. But Jesus had gone on to become a shepherd by being a servant, and His flock was a powerful deterrent against His arrest.

It was the same with the sixteenth-century reformers. Martin Luther would have been arrested and killed as soon as the Reformation began, had his service not built up a powerful popular opinion in his favour. When Miltitz, a Saxon nobleman and chamberlain in the papal court, was sent by the Pope to secure the support of Frederick the Wise (the Duke of Saxony) against Luther, he realised as he travelled through Germany that public opinion was so strongly in favour of Luther that even if he had an army at his command, he could not take Luther to Rome. The people did not stand up for Luther (or Jesus) just because he was a saint, a great preacher or a theologian, but because they could see that Luther's stand against the Roman exploitation was in their own interest.

Service is the legitimate means of acquiring the power to lead. Service done with prophetic compassion makes one a shepherd, the de facto leader of the community.

Jesus asked Peter to take care of His sheep. The Holy Spirit empowered him for that service. Paul made it clear in 1 Corinthians 12 that the power and gifts of the Holy Spirit are for service to others. 'There are different kinds of service,' he said, 'but the same Lord . . . to each one the manifestation of the Spirit is given for the common good' (vv.5–7). That is why love – the fruit of the Spirit – is the greatest power we must seek (1 Cor. 13).

Prayer: The Source of Power

The Holy Spirit empowers us for prophetic, compassionate evangelism in response to prayer. The power comes from prayer, because prayer puts us in touch with God.

In the Garden of Gethsemane, just before His arrest, Jesus asked His disciples to pray so that they might have the power to withstand opposition. They did not pray; therefore, they fled before the threat of persecution. Before His ascension, Jesus asked them again to pray; they did, and were filled with the Holy Spirit and with power to serve, to suffer and to turn the world upside-down (reform) with their prophetic preaching.

A theology of power has to begin with God, who is all powerful. When Zerubbabel, Joshua the High Priest, Ezra and Nehemiah faced the task of restoration and rebuilding, they were told by God 'Not by might nor by power, but by my Spirit' the great mountain shall be removed (Zech. 4:6). Nehemiah had to build with a sword in his hand, but the Bible makes it clear that his faith rested not in the power of the sword but in God. If there was ever a man of prayer, he was one. His power for great reforms came from prayer.

Dependence on God and the use of service, suffering, the sword or wise strategies are not mutually exclusive. It is like taking medicine and praying for healing.

Of course, some people do not even take medicines because they find it inconsistent with faith. My question to them is, 'Why do you pick up a spanner or a screwdriver to repair your bicycle when it goes wrong? Don't you believe that God can fix it? Why don't you just pray?' Their reply inevitably is, 'Because a bicycle is a machine.' But the body is also a machine, as is the universe. Just as a man can work on a bicycle, so can man work on the human body and in the physical universe. Because man is made in God's image, his actions have significance. We must not belittle man's God-given abilities and significance. But we must also remember that just as a machine is open to human intervention, so it is open to divine intervention. God can and does work in the universe, in a human body and in a machine like a bicycle. Four times I have seen a scooter and a car run on prayer! Because the universe is open to God's intervention, prayer has meaning and significance. Both prayer and wise strategies are necessary for world-transforming witness. Man forgets prayer only at his own peril.

One night the chief of village Karri came to our community to ask if any of us knew sorcery. A Brahmin woman, Ramkali, had been bitten by a snake. The sorcerers had been called and they were casting spells when she became unconscious. The Government doctor, who was there, gave her intravenous glucose, because he didn't have anti-venom. Her condition became more critical. When she was dying, her friends were running around looking for witch doctors.

I said to the chief, 'We don't know sorcery, but we can pray.' He said, 'Please come and at least pray.' Three of us Christians and one Muslim seeker went to pray. We knelt around Ramkali's bed. Over fifty people, including the doctor, watched us as we prayed for this virtually dead woman. In less than ten minutes as we opened our eyes, she did, too! On the third day she walked to our home three miles away to thank us and the living God who answers prayers.

I know that prayer is a Christian's source of power, because I have seen the power of prayer in our struggle with the Government, police, politicians, power structures of villages, 'goondas' and bandits. For months the highest police officer of Chatarpur had been threatening to kill me. For at least one year a politician of the ruling party and another of the Communist party schemed ways to kill me. But through the power of prayer, we were able to withstand all this. We have seen the power of prayer in bringing hardened people to repentance and moving believers to share their wealth with the needy at great personal cost.

I believe in human planning, strategy and action because man is significant. He affects not only machines but society and history as well. But I also believe in prayer because God is Almighty. He acts in the mechanical universe, as well as in the hearts of believers and unbelievers. I believe in prayer because God is the author and finisher of history; therefore, prayer for reformation, prayer for change in society has meaning. One of the greatest reforms in Biblical history came when men like Daniel (Dan. 9) and Nehemiah (Neh. 1) prayed.

Prayer not only has meaning but it is the only solution when we are faced with natural, social or spiritual problems which are beyond human wisdom and strength, because prayer releases the power of God.

It is necessary that we stand in the supernatural power of the Holy Spirit, because the battle between good and evil ultimately is supernatural. Modern man ignores the supernatural, diabolic dimension of evil; therefore, he is unable to understand or to deal with the social dimension of evil.

Praying is trusting God. The Bible says that faith is what ultimately overcomes the world (1 John 5:5). Faith is power because it produces hope and generates action in a stagnant society. Faith is power because it produces patience and perseverance. Faith is power because it gives staying power in the midst of opposition – the power to stand, to serve, to fight, to suffer, to die and to overcome. Most supremely, trusting or praying releases power because our dependence on God moves Him to act.

5

THE CHURCH AND SOCIAL REFORM: A POWER STRUCTURE FOR THE POOR

Social evils are sometimes unjust social relationships and their chronic consequences. The Church was meant to be a structure to ensure just relationships; therefore, by its very nature it was intended to be the answer to social evils, a force for social reform, a threat to the unjust oppression.

Poverty, when it is chronic, for example, can also be a product of oppressive, exploitative economic relations. The Proverbs say, 'A poor man's field may produce abundant food, but injustice sweeps it away' (13.23). In this chapter we shall see that in the Bible the Church is the antidote to poverty, because it was meant to be a community bound by self-sacrificing love.

In Chapter 2 we saw that slavery, i.e. oppressive, exploitative economic relationships, is justified and perpetuated by false beliefs; therefore, proclamation of truth is the basic tool of reform. Poverty, however, has not only a theological dimension to it but a social dimension also. That is the focus of our concern in this chapter.

Evangelism which does not take church planting seriously usually springs from a deficient theology which does not take the social dimensions of sin and salvation seriously. Evangelism without church planting and evangelism without a compassionate concern for society are two sides of the same coin. They are rooted in the lack of a clear understanding of the mission of our Lord.

The Mission of Christ and the Necessity of the Church

We do not need to take a comprehensive look at the mission of our Lord to understand why it was necessary for Jesus to create the Church. We can be selective and refer to only three examples of how Jesus perceived Himself, the people and His Church to understand the role of the Church.

1. Jesus's Perception of Himself

Jesus proved his Messiahship by pointing out His mission to the weak and the poor. When John the Baptist sent his disciples to find out whether Jesus was indeed the Christ, Jesus responded by exhibiting His compassion for the needy and saying, 'Go back and report to John what you have seen and heard: The blind receive sight, the lame walk, those who have leprosy are cured, the deaf hear, the dead are raised and the good news is preached to the poor.' (Luke 7:22).

According to Luke, when Jesus first claimed to be the Messiah He supported this claim from Isaiah 61:1–2.

> The Spirit of the Lord is on me,
> because he has anointed me to preach
> good news to the poor.
> He has sent me to proclaim freedom
> for the prisoners
> and recovery of sight for the blind,
> to release the oppressed,
> to proclaim the year of the Lord's favour (Luke 4:18–19).

2. Jesus's Perception of People

Jesus did not see people merely as souls to be saved from hell. He saw them as sheep without a shepherd, 'harassed and helpless' (Matt. 9:36); sheep in need of deliverance from the wolves (Matt. 10:16); as oppressed men 'weary and burdened' who needed rest (Matt. 11:28). Jesus's claim to kingship rested on the fact that He was a 'ruler who will be the shepherd of . . . Israel' (Matt. 2:6).

3. Jesus's Perception of the Church

Jesus said that He was sent 'to the lost sheep of Israel' (Matt. 15:24) to gather them into the fold, like the good shepherd who leaves the ninety-nine and goes after the one that is lost, to bring it in (Matt. 18:12–14). He sent out His disciples to do the same, to work as under-shepherds, to gather the harassed sheep into an 'ecclesia', the Church. 'As the Father has sent me,' said Jesus, 'I am sending you' (John 20:21). Why is He sending them? To take care of the sheep, who are at present at the mercy of wolves. 'Feed my lambs . . .' He gently pleaded with Simon Peter, 'Take care of my sheep . . . Feed my sheep' (John 21:15–17).

The Church as a Power Structure

Many Christians conceive of the Church as merely a harmless, worshipping, witnessing and serving community. If it were so, it hardly needed the supernatural power which we discussed in the previous chapter. When Jesus used the word 'ecclesia' to describe the community He was intending to create, He obviously had an image of the Church which is radically different from the modern connotations created by the word 'Church'. William Barclay, in his study *New Testament Words*, describes what the word 'ecclesia' meant. That was the picture which Jesus's use of the word *'Church'* would have conjured up in the minds of His audience. Barclay says:

> The ecclesia was the convened assembly of the people (in Greek City States). It consisted of all the citizens of the city who had not lost their civic rights. Apart from the fact that its

decisions must conform to the laws of the State, its powers were to all intents and purposes unlimited. It elected and dismissed magistrates and directed the policy of the city. It declared wars, made peace, contracted treaties and arranged alliances. It elected generals and other military officers. It assigned troops to different campaigns and despatched them from the city. It was ultimately responsible for the conduct of all military operations. It raised and allocated funds. Two things are interesting to note: first, all its meetings began with prayer and a sacrifice. Second, it was a true democracy. Its two great watchwords were 'equality' (*isonomia*) and 'freedom' (*eleutheria*). It was an assembly where everyone had an equal right and an equal duty to take part.*

Thus, according to Barclay, ecclesia referred to a power structure.

Did the word ecclesia have similar connotations in Jesus's mind, as described by William Barclay? Yes, in the very first usage of the word ecclesia, Jesus envisaged a community in conflict. He said to Simon, 'And I tell you that you are Peter, and on this rock I will build my church, and the gates of Hades will not overcome it' (Matt. 16:18).

In this first statement about the Church, we are told that the Church was going to be a social structure in conflict with the forces of death. Why? Because in an oppressive society if a group stands up to take care of the lambs, it automatically stands up against the wolves. The wolves are bound to fight the good shepherd. They have to do their best to destroy the ecclesia, if the ecclesia dares to protect the sheep. The Church was not meant to be an army that attacks evil, oppressive social structures, but a community that cares for the harassed and helpless sheep. But, unlike many Christians, Christ had no romantic vision of peaceful service. He knew that one cannot serve the sheep realistically without infuriating the vested interests – the wolves. Therefore, because conflict was inevitable, the Church had to be a powerful structure, a

---

*William Barclay, *New Testament Words*, SCM Press, 1964, pp. 68–9.

community that could withstand the very forces of Hades itself. It had to be a community which had the power to take up its cross, to follow its master.

The Church as the Antidote to Social Evils

Perhaps the themes of this chapter are best summed up in Ezekiel 34 which deals with the following facts:

(a) Poverty: A Product of Unjust Relationships

Poverty in Israel then was a problem of unjust economic relationships.
Ezekiel said:

> The Lord spoke to me. Mortal man, denounce the rulers of Israel. Prophesy to them, and tell them what I, the Sovereign Lord, say to them: You are doomed, you shepherds of Israel! You take care of yourselves, but never tend the sheep. You drink the milk, wear clothes made from the wool, and kill and eat the finest sheep. But you never tend the sheep. You have not taken care of the weak ones, healed the ones that are sick, bandaged the ones that are hurt, brought back the ones that wandered off, or looked for the ones that were lost. Instead, you treated them cruelly . . .
>
> Now then, my flock, I, the Sovereign Lord, tell you that I will judge each of you and separate the good from the bad, the sheep from the goats. Some of you are not satisfied with eating the best grass; you even trample down what you don't eat! You drink the clear water and muddy what you don't drink! My other sheep have to eat the grass you trample down and drink the water you muddy. So now, I, the Sovereign Lord, tell you that I will judge between you strong sheep and the weak sheep. You pushed the sick ones aside and butted them away from the flock . . . (34:1–4; 17–20).

(b) Ingathering of Sheep is the Answer to Poverty

The shepherdhood of the Messiah was seen in His care for the weak and the hungry sheep.

I, the Sovereign Lord, tell you that I myself will look for my sheep and take care of them in the same way as a shepherd takes care of his sheep that were scattered and are brought together again. I will bring them back from all the places where they were scattered . . .

I myself will be the shepherd of my sheep, and I will find them a place to rest (Ezek. 34:11–15).

(c) The Kingship of Christ as Shepherdhood

The Messiah's primary answer to socio-economic problems would be in gathering the harassed sheep into His flock.

I, the Sovereign Lord have spoken, I will look for those that are lost, bring back those that wander off, bandage those that are hurt, and heal those that are sick; but those that are fat and strong I will destroy, because I am a shepherd who does what is right . . . I will give them a king like my servant David to be their one shepherd, and he will take care of them. I, the Lord, will be their God, and a king like my servant David will be their ruler . . .

I will give them fertile fields and put an end to hunger in the land. The other nations will not sneer at them any more. Everyone will know that I protect Israel and that they are my people . . . You, my sheep, my flock that I feed, are my people, and I am your God (Ezek. 34:15–23; 29–31).

Contemporary Image of the Church

Looking at much of the contemporary Church in India, one can be justified in dismissing the view that the Church is the antidote to poverty. Shamefully, we must confess that very often the institutional Church has been the cause or means of perpetuating injustice and poverty. One ecumenical theologian, who is on the pay-roll of a church-related institution and is concerned about poverty, argued in a conference that the greatest sacrifice the Church can make for the poor in the twentieth century is to sacrifice itself, i.e., get out of existence! We have no quarrel with such theologians because they are talking about the existing image and reality of a part of the Church. In fact, we are ashamed that ecumenical theologians have had the courage to attack the evils within the Church, whereas evangelicals have sometimes been content either to woo even the corrupt Church leaders or just separate themselves from the wider Church.

The problem with these theologians begins when they seem to dismiss the very concept of Church as irrelevant to the struggle against injustice and the struggle for the weak. At that point it seems that the economists understand the need for human organisation to combat poverty better than the theologians. For example, C. T. Kurien, a leftist economist, in his book, *Poverty and Development*, says that development in India is possible only through a conscious and deliberate mass movement. He said,

> a mass movement can be effected only through organising for action and through various forms of new institutions . . . Such institutions also serve as new centres of power however limited their density may be to begin with. What is significant is that they form a new basis of power – the power of an informed and organised people as contrasted with property power, for instance. The building up of such a new power base is necessary to bring about a separation between property power and political power which so often tend to merge.*

Many people fail to see the relevance of the Church to the question of social evils such as chronic poverty, because progress is judged in terms of quantity of production. Therefore, the problem of poverty is seen as a problem of technology – lack of technical know-how, tools and material resources.

Knowledge, tools and resources are indeed important,

---

*C. T. Kurien, *Poverty and Development*, CLS, Madras, 1974, p. 24.

but their lack is not the basic problem, certainly not in rural India. A Western agriculturist, who worked for years in India trying to fight poverty at the grass-roots level with appropriate technology, ultimately gave up in despair. He said to me, 'If the problems were technological, we could have solved them, because we have all the technical answers. But the problem is different. My training and background do not enable me even to understand the problems of poverty.'

One of the basic causes of poverty is the concentration of political power in the hands of those who are also economically and socially powerful. Hinduism gives religious sanction to this concentration of power which is almost consistently used for oppression. The top leadership of the nation also uses (and thereby reinforces) the hold of the existing power structures for gathering votes. Much of the Church development also works to strengthen the existing leadership, but hardly anyone consciously stands up to empower the oppressed . . . though that is precisely what Jesus did.

From the Acts of the Apostles, we see that Jerusalem, like any other pilgrim centre, attracted the poor, orphans, widows, beggars, priests and others. These poor were attracted to the Church, because the Church was a centre of power which cared for the weak, in contrast to the Jewish temple. Once they came into the Church, they were no longer poor because the believers shared their wealth with each other very liberally. 'There were no needy persons among them,' the New Testament says. 'For from time to time those who owned lands or houses sold them, brought the money from the sales and put it at the apostles' feet, and it was distributed to anyone as he had need' (4:34–5).

This care for the powerless did not come about after Pentecost. It was part of the ministry of Christ's ecclesia during His own life. It was not just the twelve apostles whose needs were met by the common purse of Christ's community. When blind beggars, such as the one at

Jericho, received their sight, the Gospels say that 'he received sight and followed Jesus' (Luke 18:35–42), i.e. the beggar no longer begged, but lived as a part of the community of disciples.

When Jesus called disciples to follow Him, He offered to look after their material needs, too. They did not need to go back to their jobs such as fishing. Even the rich young ruler was asked to give away all his wealth and follow Jesus (Luke 18:22). The incident at the Lord's Supper makes it clear that care for the poor was a routine function of Christ's community. When Jesus told Judas, 'What you are about to do, do quickly,' His disciples thought that, 'Since Judas has charge of the money . . . Jesus was telling him . . . to give something to the poor' (John 13:27–9). Earlier, when Mary anointed Jesus's feet with expensive perfume, Judas asked, 'Why wasn't this perfume sold and the money given to the poor?' (John 12:5).

This care of the poor continued after Christ's ascension. Paul says that the Church leadership had specifically asked him to take care of the poor, which he was doing anyway (Gal. 2:10). The Church was a power structure which was intended to care for the powerless. Jesus compared the Church to a small seed which grows into a mighty tree, 'so that the birds of the air come and perch in its branches' (Matt. 13:32).

In contrast to the Jewish Establishment where political and economic power had become concentrated in the same hands, the New Testament Church was a counterbalancing centre of power. C. T. Kurien said that India needed 'a new basis of power – the power of an informed and organised people as contrasted with property power.'* To build up an ecclesia in poor societies, such as an Indian village where the present social organisation (caste) favours the powerful, is to build up a new power base which automatically threatens the concentration of political and economic power.

---

*C. T. Kurien, *Poverty and Development*, CLS, Madras, 1974, p. 24.

The evangelists who go out preaching the Good News, in obedience to their Lord, are often unaware of the social implications of conversion and church planting. Their opponents, however, understand much better the threat that the Church represents. That is why they oppose evangelism and church planting. Today in India, the most serious opposition to evangelism, conversion and church planting comes from those Hindu organisations such as the RSS and Vishwa Hindu Parishad, which are committed to re-establishing political control of the nation in the hands of the high-caste Hindus – those who already have the economic and social power. These organisations understand the political threat a growing Church represents.

To appreciate the breadth of Jesus's vision of ecclesia it will be helpful to look afresh at His statement in Matthew 16:18:

> I tell you that you are Peter, and on this rock I will build my church and the gates of Hades will not overcome it.

Church: A Community in Conflict with Forces of Death

We have already noticed the fact that Jesus implied in this statement that the Church will be a community in conflict with the forces of death because it will be a channel of life to the little lambs, which are harassed and helpless without a shepherd.

Church: A Community of Servants, not a Collection of Heroes

Peter was one of those disciples who were dreaming of sitting next to Jesus at His left or right hand when He came to power. They dreamt of the day when the present political institutions of darkness, under the authority of Satan, will be overthrown and the Kingship of Christ will be established. It was a great revolution for which they were planning to fight.

Therefore, when a few mothers brought their little children to Jesus so that He might bless them, the disciples got upset. 'Why do you make our master weary,' they probably said, 'by these petty petitions of yours? Don't you see the great mission for which we need to conserve our energies?' Jesus rebuked the disciples. 'Let the little children come to me,' He said, 'for the kingdom of heaven belongs to such as these' (Matt. 19:14).

The great people are already having good times in the kingdom of Satan. They don't need the Kingdom of God. If the Kingdom of God means nothing for these little ones, it means nothing at all.

After Peter's confession of Jesus as Messiah in Matthew 16:16, Jesus began to teach His disciples 'that He must go to Jerusalem and suffer many things at the hands of the elders, chief priests and teachers of the law, and that He must be killed . . .' (Matt. 16:21).

At this Peter was upset and began to rebuke Jesus. Peter may have said, 'what do you mean, you are going to die? Are we fools that we have left our wives and work to follow you and you want to end up on a cross? Our families have allowed us to follow you because one day they expect to see us on the throne with you. You can't desert us like that.'

Jesus responded to Peter with a severe rebuke: 'Get behind me, Satan!' (v.23).

Just because Peter acknowledged Jesus as King he did not qualify to become a hero in Christ's ecclesia. He was being called to become a servant, a shepherd to the helpless sheep and to lay down his life for the lambs.

Jesus said, 'If anyone would come after me, he must deny himself and take up his cross and follow me. For whoever wants to save his life will lose it, but whoever loses his life for me will find it' (vv.24–5).

Jesus was saying that the structure which can withstand the forces of death will not be a collection of heroes but a community of love, an ecclesia – where leaders are willing to lay down their lives for one another. That was Christ's vision of the Church.

The writers of the New Testament devote much space in their epistles, in exhorting us to be a church, a body, a temple in which God can dwell through His Spirit because there is a context of love and holiness which results in our mutual submission to one another.

Church: A Community Built on a Victorious Faith

'Upon this rock,' said Jesus, 'I will build my church . . . I will give you the keys of the kingdom of heaven; whatever you bind on earth will be bound in heaven, and whatever you loose on earth, will be loosed in heaven' (Matt. 16:18–19).

Chairman Mao taught that political power comes from the barrel of a gun. Jesus said to Peter that his knowledge of the truth that Jesus is 'Christ, the Son of the living God' (Matt. 16:16), and faith in that truth is the rock upon which the victorious ecclesia will be built.

While the angel was describing the brutal power of the kingdom of Satan to Daniel, he conceded that strength of arm will not be able to withstand the power of wickedness. 'But the people that do know their God', said the angel, 'shall be strong and do exploits (Dan. 11:32 AV) or, as the New International Version puts it, 'the people who know their God will firmly resist him' (the evil ruler).

The apostle John says, 'This is the victory that has overcome the world, even our faith. Who is it that overcomes the world? Only he who believes that Jesus is the Son of God' (1 John 5:4–5).

The Church is a community that cares for the weak, but it is built on a victorious faith. In a supernatural universe, the battle for social reform requires a transcendental faith.

Church: A Dwelling-Place of God

Jesus said, '*I will build my church*'. We have seen that the Bible teaches that the root cause of social evils is that the world has become Satan's kingdom. In contrast, Jesus is seeking to establish the Church as God's dwelling-place in the midst of the kingdom of Satan. The Church is God's new community in a fallen world, a channel of life and liberty. It is described as God's 'temple', 'household', 'bride' or the body of which Christ is the head. It is created to be the showpiece of God's work of redemption through which the manifold wisdom of God could be exhibited to the rulers and authorities in the supernatural dimensions of the universe (Eph. 3:10).

Church: An Inseparable Part of the Good News

Upon this victorious faith . . . '*I will build my church, and the gates of Hades will not overcome it*' means that the creation of the Church is an intrinsic part of the hope, the Good News that Jesus offers. The Good News is a message of individual forgiveness for sin, freedom from captivity of enslaving beliefs – and it is also the creation of a new community, built on truth, which cares for others with self-sacrificing love – a community which overcomes sinful social barriers that alienate men such as Jews v. Gentiles, masters v. slaves, men v. women.

St Paul says that the Church is:

the mystery of Christ, which was not made known to men in other generations as it has now been revealed by the Spirit to

God's holy apostles and prophets. This mystery is that through the gospel the Gentiles are heirs together with Israel, members together of one body, and sharers together in the promise in Christ Jesus (Eph. 3:4–6).

St Paul was excited about the Church, 'the great mystery of God', because the Church is the 'unsearchable riches of Christ . . . in God'.

The Church can become a matter of excitement in a country like India if it is seen to be uniting 'untouchables' and the 'high caste' into one body. The same applies to other countries where human beings are sharply divided according to race, colour, economic status, sex, etc. These alienations are the results of sin, features of the kingdom of Satan. Salvation includes becoming one body by overcoming the sin that separates.

An Unfinished Story

In 1980, as a result of the work of ACRA, three small worshipping congregations had sprung up, consisting exclusively of non-Christians who had put their trust in Christ. In one village five families, led by my father, used to meet for worship. 'D' was one of them – a semi-literate man converted from an untouchable background. Some years ago, when he was a child, his family land had been forcibly taken by a high-caste Hindu. In 1974, while 'D' was still a Hindu, he started a court case against the man who had grabbed his land. The case did not go far because no one in the village was willing to come forward as a witness in support of 'D'. This was because twenty-five families had grabbed the little plots that had been given to over 100 families. The twenty-five families were more powerful than the 100 families. Therefore, the poor could not even give witness for one another.

But the Church was a new factor in that oppressive situation. 'D' shared his problem with other Christians and they prayed about it. They felt that the case should be reopened. After some time the Church discovered that legally the land still belonged to 'D'; he just needed the courage to cultivate it. The prayer and moral support of the little church gave him the courage to venture out and repossess his land. Another believer, 'S', from the same village offered to plough the land for 'D' with our tractor. The high-caste man's family stood by with their axes, abusing us and threatening to murder 'S'. But because they feared that the other church members would bear witness in court, they did not take any step. The next day they said, 'You have ploughed the land, but we will sow it.' That night 'S' took the tractor and sowed the field himself. The high caste were infuriated.

They called a meeting of high-caste Hindus from nearly thirty villages to discuss what to do with these Christians. The high-caste man who had grabbed 'D's land argued convincingly that it was not a matter of one man and his land, but of thousands of acres belonging to thousands of low castes. He said, 'If one of these untouchables succeeded in getting his land back, with the help of the Christians, you can be sure that thousands of them will become Christians and we shall lose our lands.' Those who participated in the meeting vowed with 'Ganga Jal' (water of the river Ganges) that they would chase the Christians away from their area. They understood the threat which the Church posed, merely by virtue of its commitment to stand with one of its weak members.

My father was threatened, 'You tell your son not to meddle in our affairs, otherwise the consequences for you will be bad.' We prayed and felt that it was worth taking the consequences. If we failed, we failed. But if we succeeded then it could open up floodgates – thousands of oppressed and thousands of acres of land.

My wife and I were leaving for a lecture-cum-study trip to Europe for three months. The night before we left, three men entered my father's farmhouse. They beat him up as well as my stepmother and tied them up. They looted the house. Then one of them threatened to gouge out my father's eyes with a knife. He did not do it because my father promised to empty out his bank account the following day and give them all his life's savings.

My father came to see us in the morning. He was worried that the men might have come to us after leaving them. He did not say a word about the incident, but as we left for the airport, he excused himself and went to the bank to draw out the money for them.

My father had to flee from the village and take temporary shelter in the city. But he was shattered. Two days later, two Hindu neighbours of 'S' were murdered over a land dispute. This shook 'S'. Then 'D' was threatened with murder. A little later my aunt and her husband were brutally murdered in their own home in Chatarpur where my father was staying. This last episode apparently did not have anything to do with our struggle, but the cumulative impact of it all was that the little church was thoroughly demoralised. Under pressure 'D' agreed to 'sell' the land to the high-caste man. The high-caste man's illegal possession was legalised for a paltry sum of three hundred rupees.

My father took a loan from ACRA and helped 'D' to buy another plot of land in the same village. It was a witness to the Church's care and commitment to the oppressed, even though it was also an admission of powerlessness and failure. 'D' is still there cultivating. For the moment the Church stands disintegrated. It is a reminder of Moses' abortive attempt in Egypt to free the Israelites. By himself he was too weak to stand against the forces of Hades. He was forced to flee. But that was not the end of the story. Moses met with God. He was transformed into a prophet and he returned and liberated the Jews in the power of God.

The above story has not ended yet. 'D' has land of his own, with an irrigation well. The bank financed him to buy an electric pump. He works hard, but cannot feed his family. In 1983 his total produce sold for less than four thousand rupees. He repaid two thousand to the bank for the pump, fertilisers, etc; twelve hundred were spent on seed, repairs and fencing. That left him with eight hundred for his annual wages, i.e., sixty-six rupees ($6) per month for a family of six. His girls were getting free education in a Christian boarding-school. He couldn't pay their travel from home to school, so in disgust he withdrew them from the school. He sold firewood to make a little extra money, but he was still forced to borrow, just to eat.

The high-caste man who grabbed 'D's land and had my father nearly killed, is our 'friend' now. Recently, with 'D' and 'S' he spent a whole day in one of our spiritual retreats listening to the Gospel. He knows that even though we disapprove of what he did, we love him and are concerned about the fact that he, too, is enslaved and exploited by the politico-economic system in which he lives. He knows that we understand that he, too, is not making ends meet and is therefore forced to exploit his neighbours, labourers, cattle, land, forest and his own children. He now knows that the Christians are as much concerned for his salvation as for 'D's.

6

CHRISTIAN HOPE AND SOCIAL REFORM: A FAITH THAT OVERCOMES THE WORLD

The evangelicals of William Carey's generation believed that the darkness would not overcome the light (John 1:5) and that a little leaven of the Gospel would transform the whole dough (Matt. 13:3). Therefore, they had the motivation to resist evils in their society. Today, however, much of the Church suffers from an eschatological paralysis: we are robbed of all meaningful motivation to challenge evils, by the prevalent belief that darkness will continue to grow till the end of history, even though we continue to launch new multimillion pound projects to spread the light.

The terrible 'success' of Fascism, Nazism, and Communism in our century, and two world wars, have destroyed all secular hopes for the future of mankind as it is. Much of the Church has read the Scriptures with that pessimistic outlook of our age and baptised it with theological rationale. We simply mourn the coming destruction of 'The Late Great Planet Earth' instead of seeking to redeem it.

The evangelicals of the earlier era had hope for man and his planet because they believed that far from abandoning this world, God, who is faithful to His word and His creation, had made a covenant with this planet. The eternal, infinite God had personally entered the finite, space–time world of fallen man with His salvation. The Kingdom of God had broken the kingdoms of this world and the gates of Hades will not overcome it (Matt. 16:18).

For them, Christian hope was not beyond history, but within it.

What exactly is the Biblical view of the future? Does the Bible give a valid basis for hope in history? What are the implications of the Christian view of the future?

A Realist's Case Against Hope

If you were to visit Bundelkhand, the area where I serve, some of my critics will tell you 'if Vishal is starting a project, it is bound to fail.' There is much substance in their assessment. My record of many failures is a very real reason for me to be pessimistic about my future efforts. Various factors are responsible for my failures and some of them lie outside my control. But some of the causes without question lie in my own limitations, ignorance and sinfulness. So, when my finiteness, foolishness and sinfulness have been conclusively established, how can I reasonably hope that my efforts or the efforts of other finite and sinful men will create a better future in our situation?

Some other critics will tell you that 'Vishal is a good fellow, and reasonably capable, but he has not been able to find good co-workers. Everyone he trusts lets him down; so his rate of success is very little compared to his investment and efforts.' Correct again! Any number of resourceful and gifted people can testify that all their efforts have come to nothing because of the personal limitations or selfishness of their colleagues and successors. Given the quality of the material one has to work with, can I realistically have any hope for the future? 'None – whatsoever', is the assessment of some who have observed our efforts.

Others of my critics, who are more sympathetic, will say to you, 'The soil here is very bad, you can't do anything with it.' Meaning: 'The people you are seeking to serve have themselves become so bad that they will use their benefactors as long as they can and then they will abuse them. They will never support them at personal cost. And because benefactors cannot achieve much without the active, sacrificial support of the local people, there is no hope.' True again! Some soils produce much fruit, others nothing. The worst soils demand the best efforts, and yet tend to give you only disappointments. The cynics are not necessarily those who have not tried, but often those who have tried hard and failed.

My well-wishers in the area may say to you, 'Vishal has done here what no one else has. But the powers that rule this area have a deeply entrenched vested interest in the status quo. They are cruel and well-armed. They will not allow a centre of power to emerge in their territory that changes the system to the advantage of "the weary and the heavy laden." The chief minister of the state himself depends on these powers and principalities. Therefore, in some of the villages the government itself has not been able to open schools for forty years, as education will undermine the present power equations. In many villages where schools have opened, the teachers survive only because they agree not to educate the children from low-caste families. So, where the government can do nothing, what can these unarmed social workers achieve? They have burnt down Vishal's community once and if he becomes a threat to the existing power structures, they will not hesitate in eliminating him.' What hope indeed can there be for a society where wickedness rules?

Even if I were not as foolish and sinful as I am; my co-workers were better than I in every respect; if the people I am seeking to serve were fearless, self-sacrificing participants in my efforts, and if the power structures at local, state and national level were supportive of actions for development – shall I succeed? Shall I then have a basis to be an optimist? Wouldn't an earthquake, a famine, an epidemic or a flood wipe away all that I create? Viewed from the macro-level, how can I have any confidence that the coming decades will not produce another Hitler or Idi Amin, or an enemy armed to the teeth with nuclear weapons? Wouldn't all our labours then be in vain? Isn't it foolish to be optimistic about the future, given the track record of mankind in recent and past history? Add to this list the new man-made environmental hazards from acid rain and deforestation, destroying the lungs of the world, to chlorofluorocarbons (CFCs) and the thinning of the ozone layer in the stratosphere, making organic life on this planet vulnerable to the sun's harmful ultraviolet radiation (the so-called 'greenhouse effect'). You have an almost irrefutable case against hope.

The Christian Case for Hope

Peter had every right to be cynical that morning. He had laboured the whole night and caught no fish. He was irritated and tired. He wanted to go home and sleep, if possible without being seen by his family, who were waiting for the fish − so that one member could start cooking the day's meal, while another went to sell the rest. But Jesus enters the scene of failure and asks Peter to lend Him the boat to serve as a pulpit for a while. Peter consents, partly because it gives him an excuse to delay the moment of embarrassment, of reaching his expectant family without fish.

After His sermon, Jesus asks Peter to take the boat into the deep and cast his net just once more. Perhaps Jesus wanted to pay for His use of the boat, but He also wanted to show that in spite of Peter's own failures, there was hope with God. 'What does this carpenter-preacher know about fishing?' would have been the natural response of Peter's professional pride. But Peter says, 'Master, I have worked hard the whole night. I have failed repeatedly and therefore I have lost hope. But I will obey you.' In that single attempt of obedience Peter caught two boatloads of fish. Divine intervention gives success in a situation of repeated failure.

The crowd had been with Jesus for three days. Their food had gone, and they were hungry. Jesus asks His disciples to feed the 5,000-strong crowd. 'How?' they wonder. A little boy then surrenders his five loaves and two fish to Jesus. They are blessed and broken. Multitudes are satisfied because divine intervention multiplies the meagre sacrifice that man can offer.

The master of the banquet was panicking because the wine was over – what a disgrace it would be to send the guests away unsatisfied! Jesus's mother pleads for His intervention. The servants are told to obey Him. They fill the jars with water. Divine intervention transforms the water of human effort into a choice wine.

Jesus could have asked Peter to close his eyes for a moment and filled his boat with fish; He could have filled the disciples' baskets with a meal or the jars at Cana with wine; all miraculously materialised. But instead He required the physical effort of casting the net again, a man's sacrifice of his own food, the human obedience of filling the jars with water. In a situation of hopelessness it was human efforts of obedience and faith that were blessed with success. Therefore, while it is right to look at my failures realistically, it is wrong not to trust and obey. With Jesus there is hope in spite of my failures.

Jesus knew He could not trust the crowd which said it trusted Him (John 2:23). But could He entrust His mission to His disciples? Weren't they totally selfish in their ambitions to sit at His right and His left? Weren't they worldly in their values when they rebuked the mothers who brought their children to Jesus for His blessings? Weren't they carnal when they debated who was the greatest among them? Weren't they too weak in their flesh to stay awake with Him in His moment of trial in Gethsemane? And too timid to confess Him before a girl in the High Priest's home? Didn't one of them betray Him for thirty pieces of silver while others fled to save their lives when He faced the cross? Indeed, the material He had to work with inspired no hope. Yet He knew that these same weak, good-for-nothing men could receive power when the Holy Ghost came upon them and then they could turn the world upside-down. Because God's power is available for weak men, there is hope.

Jesus knew well that the sheep will not lay down their lives for their shepherd. It is the shepherd's responsibility to lay down his life for their sake. He knew that the sheep would all be scattered when the shepherd was slain (Matt. 26:31). Woe unto us if we seek to serve the sheep in the hope of some returns from them. The Scriptures say, 'Cursed is the one who trusts in man' (Jer. 17:5). How can the sheep who cannot save themselves save the shepherd? Yet, if the shepherd truly loves them, and is willing to lay down his life for them, they will follow him (John 10:15). A grain of wheat will abide alone until it falls to the ground and dies. But if it dies, Jesus said, it will bring forth much fruit (John 12:24). So while it is true that one cannot have hope if he looks to his co-workers or the beneficiaries of his service, yet faith in God and willingness to obey unto death provide solid foundations for hope.

In our conflicts with powers and principalities, I have lost many co-workers because they looked too closely at the power of the wickedness they were up against. The strength and cruelty of the enemy overwhelmed them and some chose to join what appeared to them to be the stronger side, while others left the battlefield.

These co-workers have always reminded me of Saruman in Tolkien's trilogy, *The Lord of the Rings*. He was a mighty wizard and knew that he should not look at the crystal ball Palantir, but he did and saw the evil eye. When he saw the awesome power of wickedness he became terrified by the power of wickedness, and he joined the evil side. In contrast Gandalf, another wizard, refused to look at the stone. He kept his sight focused on the power of truth. The little hobbits have been my favourite heroes. Oblivious of the power of wickedness and the great perils that awaited them at every turn, their only concern was to obey their call, so they kept walking in the midst of fearsome dangers, protected by unseen forces. That is a beautiful picture of Christian warfare. A person who looks too closely at principalities and powers will be frightened. He will have no reasonable basis for hope just as ten of the twelve spies that Moses sent to scout the promised land concluded that they could not possibly win. It takes a Joshua to conquer the promised land because he looks not at the power of the enemy but at the commander of the armies of the Lord (Josh. 5:13–15); and therefore is willing just to walk around the impenetrable walls of Jericho; and raise the shouts of praise and victory by faith (Josh. 6).

The inevitability of death, whether through old age or nuclear holocaust is the ultimate logical cause for pessimism. Death and decay make all human endeavours futile, even absurd. Fear of death is the ultimate weapon of the kingdom of Satan (Heb. 2:14–15). If you threaten the rule of wickedness in a social system, the maximum it can do to protect itself is to eliminate you. By His death and resurrection, however, Jesus has destroyed Satan's final weapon. He was not only raised from the dead but was exalted to the highest position of authority in the universe. 'All authority,' said Jesus, 'is given unto me in heaven and on earth' (Matt. 28:18). His victory over death in history is therefore the ultimate foundation of hope for this world. Jesus is only the 'first fruit' of resurrection, the Bible says; God will destroy death – the last enemy (1 Cor. 15:26). And we will rise with Him to eternal life. Not only human beings, but 'the creation itself will be liberated from its bondage to decay and brought into the glorious freedom of the children of God' (Rom. 8:21).

Jesus who rose again bodily from the dead, who ascended into heaven and is exalted above all principalities and powers, is coming back to earth to judge and to rule. This gives the final basis for hope to a Christian.

But it is tragic that in our age, this doctrine of hope – the second coming of Christ – has been read with the pessimistic outlook of the secular world and turned into the final basis for 'Christian' pessimism.

A Hindu views God as Creator (Brahma), sustainer (Vishnu) and destroyer (Shiva). But the Bible presents

God as the Creator, Saviour and judge – not destroyer. A
judge, in the Bible, is someone who punishes the wicked
and establishes justice on earth. That is a message of hope
for a man who chooses to suffer for righteousness' sake in
an age where wickedness is the way to prosper.

In Revelation, chapter 6, John sees the souls of the
martyrs who ask God, 'How long . . . until you judge the
inhabitants of the earth and avenge our blood?' (v.10). Is it
in vain, they ask, that we chose the path of righteousness,
refused to compromise with evil, and lost our heads? Was
it worth sacrificing our families, properties, pleasures and
life for truth? They are assured that it was all worth it
because God will visit the earth in judgment.

The Scriptures say that Jesus will return with the fire of
judgment.

> . . . the present heavens and earth are reserved for fire, being
> kept for the day of judgment and destruction of ungodly men
> . . . the day of the Lord will come like a thief. The heavens will
> disappear with a roar; the elements will be destroyed by fire
> and the earth and everything in it will be laid bare [i.e. found]
> . . . But in keeping with His promise we are looking forward to
> a new heaven and a new earth, the home of righteousness
> (2 Pet. 3:7, 10, 13).

This passage, which is meant to give a warning to the
wicked and hope to the saints, has been read by many
Christians in such a way that it takes away all hope for the
social and physical world in history.

We need to realise, first of all, that the background of
Peter's teaching here is the prophesy of Malachi: 'Then
suddenly the Lord you are seeking will come to His temple
. . . But who can endure the day of His coming? Who can
stand when He appears? For He will be like a refiner's fire
or a launderer's soap. He will sit as a refiner and purifier of
silver' (Mal. 3:1–3).

The fire Scripture is talking about is refiner's fire which
burns up the dross and purifies the silver. The fire is for

'the destruction of the ungodly men' and 'the elements'. The word *elements* does not refer to the elements of physical earth which are the building blocks of our planet. The Greek for *elements* that Peter uses here is *stoicheia* which is also used in Galatians 4:3, 9 where it is translated as 'basic principles of the world' and 'those weak and miserable principles', and in Colossians 2:8, 20 where it is translated as 'basic principles of this world' which are 'hollow and deceptive philosophy, which depends on human tradition' and enslaves people. The word 'elements' thus refers not to the elements of modern chemistry but of Greek thought which even has connotations of stars and spirits of astrology that control men. Thus, according to Peter, the fire of the Lord will burn up the 'ungodly men' and their enslaving religious principles that result in wickedness and hostility to God.

Some versions do translate 2 Peter 3:10 as 'the elements will be destroyed by fire, and the earth and everything in it will be *burned* up'. But most modern translations of the Bible use the phrase 'laid bare' or the more literal translation, 'found' instead of burned up. Because 'found' is the literal meaning of the Greek word *heuretesetai* which is the word used by Peter, according to the Sinaiticus and Vaticanus manuscripts of the New Testament. The word 'found' in the phrase 'earth will be found' is the same joyous word used in the parable of the prodigal son, 'my son was lost but is now found', or in the parable which says that the Kingdom of God is like a man who found a pearl of great value. So what Peter is saying in 2 Peter 3:10 is not that the earth will be burnt up, but that the ungodly men and the basic teachings of the world that hold this world in captivity to sin and death, will be burnt up and the earth will be refined and restored to its original status.

This interpretation of 2 Peter 3:10 is the consistent way of interpreting the text in its context. In chapters 2 and 3 Peter relates the coming judgment with fire to the previous judgment with fire, which was not destruction of the world in the Hindu sense, but in the sense of judgment

122

which purifies. Peter in concluding his teaching on this subject again uses the word 'found' in the sense of refined and found.

'Since everything will be destroyed in this way, what kind of people ought you to be? . . . since you are looking forward to this [as a positive hope], make every effort to be found spotless, blameless and at peace with him' (2 Pet. 3:11–14). This positive view of the future is also taught by Paul in Romans 8:19–21:

> The creation waits in eager expectation for the sons of God to be revealed. For the creation was subjected to frustration, not by its own choice, but by the will of the one who subjected it, in hope that the creation itself will be liberated from its bondage to decay and brought into the glorious freedom of the children of God.

Peter does not contradict Paul's teachings in his second epistle, but confirms them. He says:

> Bear in mind that our Lord's patience [in delaying judgment] means salvation, just as our dear brother Paul also wrote to you with the wisdom that God gave him. He writes the same way in all his letters, speaking in them of these matters. His letters contain some things that are hard to understand which ignorant and unstable people distort as they do the other Scriptures to their own destruction (2 Peter 3:15–16).

This translation of 2 Peter 3:10*b*, that the earth will be 'found', is also in harmony with verse 13 which says that we are looking forward to a *new earth*. The word *new* is not *neos* which means 'brand new' but *Kainos* which means '*renewed*'. All that was created as '*good*' will be retained and restored.*

This earth will not disappear, but will be given to the meek as their inheritance (Matt. 5:5). We shall not live in

*For a detailed Bible study on this subject please see Dr Wim Rietkerk's book, *The Future Great Planet Earth*, to be published by Nivedit Good Books Distributors (CP) Ltd, Landour, Mussoorie, U.P., India.

heaven for ever, but the mansions that Jesus is preparing in heaven (John 14:2) will come down to earth (Rev. 21:2). We shall not live as disembodied spirits. But the dead shall rise again with glorified, non-perishable bodies (1 Cor. 15:51–5) and God Himself will dwell on earth with His saints (John 14:23; Rev. 21:3). The physical creation will not disappear, but:

> The wilderness and dry land shall be glad, the desert shall rejoice and blossom; like the crocus it shall blossom abundantly, and rejoice with joy and singing (Isa. 35:1–2 RSV).

Nor will the animals be absent in the new earth:

> The wolf shall dwell with the lamb, and the leopard shall lie down with the kid, and the calf and the lion and the fatling together, and a little child shall lead them . . . The sucking child shall play over the hole of the asp; and the weaned child shall put his hand on the adder's den (Isa. 11:6–9 RSV).

It is not the souls of the saints that will live with Jesus, but the nations of this world:

> He shall judge between the nations, and shall decide for many peoples; and they shall beat their swords into ploughshares, and their spears into pruning hooks; nation shall not lift up sword against nation, neither shall they learn war any more (Isa. 2:4).

On the other hand, in the new earth:

> The nations will walk by its [God's city's] light, and the kings of the earth will bring their splendour into it. On no day will its gates ever be shut, for there will be no night there. The glory and honour of the nations will be brought into it (Rev. 21:24–6).

The city of God will have a river of the water of life and on each side of the river there will be the tree of life.

And the leaves of the tree are for the healing of the nations.
No longer will there be any curse (Rev. 22:2–3).

There is hope for this planet, its deserts and trees, for its
Creator is faithful to His creation. He remembers His
covenant not to destroy it:

Then God said to Noah and to his sons with him: 'I now
establish my covenant with you and with your descendants
after you and with every living creature that was with you –
the birds, the livestock and all the wild animals, all those that
came out of the ark with you – every living creature on earth.
I establish my covenant with you: Never again will all life be
cut off by the waters of a flood; never again will there be a flood
to destroy the earth (Gen. 9:8–11).

The late Dr Francis Schaeffer often used to say 'man is lost
but he is not zero.' Hinduism makes Self (God) the only
reality and both man (self) and the physical world zero,
i.e., Maya or a projection of universal consciousness; like a
dream that can be both created and destroyed. Much of
modern scientific thought also reduces man to zero – a
mere machine or an animal. The behavioural school of
psychology denies that man is a person who makes real
choices. He is no different from a machine where everything is determined by external causes. Likewise, the
view that the universe is not the work of a personal
creator, but a product of random chance and impersonal
energy make the physical world zero. The Christian view,
on the other hand, that the physical universe and man are
both works of a personal creator who declared them to be
good and who is faithful to His creation, puts great value
on both man and the earth.

Man is not zero. But he is a sinner. The earth is not zero,
but is cursed because of man's sin. God is not destroyer,
but a judge who will punish sin and destroy all the
consequences of sin, because He seeks to redeem His
creation. This is a message of great hope for the future of

this earth. Not only the earth, but Paul says that even believers will go through refiner's fire:

> If any man builds on this foundation using gold, silver, costly stones, wood, hay or straw, his work will be shown for what it is, because the Day will bring it to light. It will be revealed with fire, and the fire will test the quality of each man's work. If what he has built survives, he will receive his reward. If it is burned up, he will suffer loss; he himself will be saved, but only as one escaping through the flames (1 Cor. 3:12–15).

That the fire of God will consume all that is sinful in me and in the world is not a message of doom, but of hope which should make us work to build things that will last for eternity. The fact that our works of beauty and value will be refined and will last, must cause us to thank God.

> We give thanks to you, Lord God Almighty,
> the One who is and who was,
> because you have taken your great power
> and have begun to reign.
> The nations were angry;
> and your wrath has come.
> The time has come for judging the dead,
> and for rewarding your servants
> the prophets and your saints
> and those who reverence your name,
> both small and great –
> and for destroying those who
> destroy the earth (Rev. 11:17–18).

The Significance of Human Action

The Christian's hope for a better future rests not on his own record of success, but on Christ's victory over sin, Satan and death in history, and on His promise to return as judge and ruler.

Does that make human action insignificant and

irrelevant? No, because the purpose of God's saving action
is to restore man's dominion on earth. The consequence of
Adam's sin was that man who was meant to be the ruler
became a slave on earth, not only to Satan and sin, but to
nature as well. The earth began to grow thorns and
thistles and he had to eat of the sweat of his brow. In his
struggle with nature, man ultimately lost, died and became dust. Physical nature won over its ruler – man.
Death became the master. But by defeating death and
giving eternal life to those who repent and believe, God is
restoring to man his authority over the world. Jesus did
not come to take our souls to Heaven, but to restore the
kingdom to us. Saints do go to Heaven when they die. But
they wait there to return with Christ to rule on this earth.
Heaven is a waiting-room until the great restoration. The
purpose of salvation is to make us kings and priests, or the
'royal priesthood' as Peter puts it (1 Pet. 2:9). Man is given
the task to rule. He had lost the kingdom and become a
slave. Jesus saves us from sin and gives us His authority to
rule.

As the elders and the heavenly creatures sing to the
lamb of God:

> You are worthy to take the scroll
> and to open its seals,
> because you were slain,
> and with your blood you
> purchased men for God
> from every tribe and language and
> people and nation.
> You have made them to be
> a kingdom and priests to
> serve our God,
> and they will reign on earth (Rev. 5:9–10).

The Christians' future is not to worship God in heaven
through eternity, but to reign on earth. Paul says that we
who were dead in trespasses and sins have already been

raised to life and made to sit with Christ in a position of authority to do good works (Eph. 2:1–10). A believer, therefore, has the responsibility to exercise his authority in his situation. As my friend Chandrakant Shourie says, when Israel stood before the Red Sea, the angel of the Lord who was going ahead of them, went behind them to protect them from Pharaoh's army. The angel in a pillar of fire would not let them go back, but in front of them was the sea. They were trapped. God did not ask the angel to divide the sea. The rod of authority was placed in man's hand. Moses was asked to raise the rod over the sea. Man has to act in obedience and faith. It could be that Moses had to hold the rod over the seas a whole night, for it says:

> Then Moses stretched out his hand over the sea, and all that night the Lord drove the sea back with a strong east wind and turned it into dry land. The waters were divided, and the Israelites went through the sea on dry ground (Exod. 14:21–22).

God is the one who delivers us from slavery. But He has given the rod of authority to man. Man has to act in obedience of faith if he wants to see God's power to deliver.

Witnesses not Revolutionaries

If God is the deliverer then man is primarily a witness to divine deliverance, not the Saviour Himself. But to witness does not mean to live on a 'spiritual' plane, removed from the realities of daily life. To bear witness to the kingship of Christ is to pick up a fight with the prince of death, who wishes to keep this world in bondage to decay.

After His resurrection the disciples asked Jesus, 'Lord, are you at this time going to restore the kingdom to Israel?' (Acts 1:6). They had seen themselves as failures. Earlier they had promised to fight for His Kingdom. Now they knew that they couldn't. So if the Kingdom had to

come, it had to be God's action – '*are you* at this time going
to restore the kingdom?' It is tragic that often the Christians who take our future hope most seriously choose to
spend their time in trying to figure out the time of His
arrival, instead of seeking to become witnesses of His
Kingship.

Jesus replies, 'It is not your job to sit back and try to find
out the timetable of my return. I know you do not have the
power to challenge the kingdom of Satan. But you will
receive power when the Holy Spirit has come upon you.
Then *you will have a role to play*. You will go out with my
authority to the uttermost parts of the world and bear
witness to my kingship.'

APPENDIX:

YOU CAN SERVE THE POOR WITHOUT GIVING AWAY YOUR MONEY

Deena was an untouchable, poverty-stricken landless man when he heard about Jesus a few years ago. He committed his life to Christ together with four others from his village. A little congregation was born and it helped him get a small plot of land. Gradually Deena was helped by other Christians to dig a well, borrow a pair of oxen and start farming.

On April 13th, 1984, he came to me and said, 'Brother, the Government has fixed the price of grain at 250 rupees per quintal [100 kg], but nobody in the market is prepared to give me more than 235 rupees. What should I do?'

'Don't sell it,' I advised him.

'Brother,' he said, 'my wife has been asking me to get her a new sari, because the only one she has is torn to shreds. I therefore have to sell this grain, so that I can get her the sari. Though, in fact, I need to keep it for food and seed. If I don't return home with the sari, she will be deeply hurt.'

'Well, listen to me,' I insisted. 'Don't sell the grain.'

A friend of mine took the bag of grain to the warehouse, and deposited it there. Then he took the warehouse receipt for the bag, and pledged it to the State Bank of India as security, and arranged with them to give Deena a loan of 237 rupees.

Three months later an excited Deena stopped me on the highway and said that the warehouse manager had advised him to sell his bag of grain as the price had now gone up from 235 to 450 rupees per quintal. Deena had used 237 rupees so he could not release his bag. We had to advance the cash. After paying 11 rupees' interest to the bank, he earned 202 rupees extra on one bag of grain.

A village that sells 1,000 bags of grain would have earned $202 \times 1,000 = 202,000$ rupees. The village would then need neither the donor agencies nor the Government to start a school, a health-care centre or a drinking-water project. It would have the money to purchase the services it needs and thus become self-sustaining.

In 1984, we were able to persuade the Agricultural Development branch of the State Bank of India to finance twenty other poor farmers like Deena. Soon some powerful people saw the enormous economic potential of this scheme in favour of the poor and so they exerted political pressure on the bank manager who stopped financing the scheme. The bank also felt that all small peasants would see the advantage of the scheme and would flood them with applications for credit against their grain. The bank would not be able to cope with the paperwork required to lend to thousands of farmers.

In 1985 we persuaded another bank to finance the farmers; however, we are afraid that this bank's management will also give in to the political pressures (because it, too, is nationalised), bribes (which the merchants will no doubt offer), and just the pressure of increased work.

So we are now forced to build up our own revolving fund to finance the poor, and we want to do it without putting any burden on your budget, through the scheme.

Serve While You Save

Many agencies come to you with appeals for money for development projects, but we are inviting you to participate in a movement of service to the poor while you save for your future.

'Is that possible?' Our answer is an emphatic 'Yes!'

Twelve years of direct involvement with the poor in India have convinced us.

Development Is an Issue of Justice Not of Charity

As the Bible says, 'A poor man's field may produce abundant food, but injustice sweeps it away' (Prov. 13:23).

The small farmer in India is poor and lives at or below the subsistence level because he rarely recovers his production cost. He is forced to sell his wheat (for example) at 162 rupees per bag (100 kg or 200 lb), whereas the production cost is approximately 262 rupees per bag. The farmer makes no money and is therefore unable to pay the necessary minimum wages to the hired labourers. Yet the business community and the Government make anywhere between 50 to 200 rupees per bag of wheat. The farmer who cannot make ends meet is forced to exploit not only his labourers, but his land, forest, cattle, family and his own body also. During the British Raj, cotton produced by the Indian farmer was purchased at an extremely low price and taken to the mills in England. The mill-made cloth was then resold in India at a high profit, taking the wealth of India back to England at the expense of the poor primary producers in India. We called it injustice, exploitation and slavery; historians called it Pax Britannica!

National independence in 1947 changed the situation only slightly. The first planning commission was persuaded by the Russian example, that India could accumulate the capital for industrialisation only if it did not pay remunerative prices for agricultural produce, i.e., if it exploited 80 per cent of its population. This policy has continued to this day. Each harvest has been used to transfer money from the field to the factory, from the village to the city, from the poor to the rich. This is PAX INDIANA! During the decade of 1971–81 alone £22,500 million have been transferred from the agricultural to the non-agricultural sector. Because this transfer has taken place not through savings and investment, but through a socialistic strategy of force and fraud, the capital is gone, but the population has remained on the land. The peasants have simply become poorer.

The grip of the rich over the economic system has become so strong now that to break these chains of slavery and to liberate the poor from this unjust exploitation will require nothing less than a nationwide movement on the scale of the independence struggle. But let us first look at the microscopic level of 1,200 villages in Chatarpur district of Madhya Pradesh, where the writer has been directly involved with the poor since 1976.

The reason I insisted that Deena should not sell his grain after the harvest in 1984 was because of what I had seen happen the previous year. In 1983, the Government had announced the 'support price' of grain to be 235 rupees per bag. When the farmers brought the grain to the procurement centre during the day, they were usually told, 'Sorry – the cash has not come yet.' Instead of taking the grain back to the village, the farmers preferred to sell it to the merchants at 180 rupees per bag, because they could not be sure that they would get the 'support price' even if they returned the next day. In the evenings, the merchants passed on the grain to the procurement centre at 235 rupees per bag, sharing the profit of 55 rupees a bag with officials.

Later in the year, the Government sold the grain at the wholesale rate of 365–390 rupees per bag, making a further profit of 145 a bag. Then the merchants sold the same grain at 425–450 rupees a bag. A Government officer said to me, 'The MP Government has earned hundreds of millions on grain.' On a million bags, the total net profit of the Government and the merchants works out to be more than 200 million rupees. This is profit. What the farmers get is not even the production cost. Is there any wonder then that the city is now mushrooming with videos and TVs whereas so many villages have no drinking water, no roads, no school buildings or even first aid clinics? The village folk still drink contaminated water and wear rags.

This enslavement of the poor by the rich, of the village by the city, is as evil as any colonialism ever was. It makes us ashamed. It moves us to call for a new national struggle for justice to the poor. What can be done about this injustice? Distributing charity or technology is certainly no answer. Increasing productivity through development projects will not help. The need is to change the unjust system and oppressive ideology that under-girds the system. As the Bible says, God's desire for us is 'to loose the chains of injustice and untie the cords of the yoke, to set the oppressed free and break every yoke' (Isa. 58:6).

THE PROPOSAL

About a thousand farmers in Chatarpur, who were badly hurt by a hailstorm in 1982, and then treated callously by the politicians and officials, initiated a peasants' organisation with ACRA's assistance. It has taken up the warehousing project as its main programme. It has streamlined the procedure for warehousing the grain, giving credit to farmers and marketing the grain. What we need is a capital fund from which immediate credit can be given to the farmers without their having to waste days queuing up in banks. This is where we need your participation. We are looking for people who will put in at least £500 each on a seven-year term deposit, in a bank in India. According to the Government regulations non-Indians can also participate in this if they deposit the money through a trust or investment company which is 60 per cent controlled by non-resident Indians. Some of our Indian friends in England have created the Indian Groundworks Trust to meet this need. An investment company is yet to be created.

The bank will give 11 per cent interest to Indians and 12 per cent interest to non-resident Indians and non-Indians who deposit through the Groundworks Trust or an investment company. We request that the depositors take 8–10 per cent interest and give the rest for the administrative expenses of the Indian Groundworks Trust. After seven years you will receive your deposit with interest, but meanwhile you would have empowered the powerless to set themselves free from the chains of injustice and the yoke of oppression.

> Then my soul will rejoice in the Lord
> and delight in His salvation.

My whole being will exclaim,
'Who is like you, O Lord?
You rescue the poor from
those too strong for them,
the poor and needy from those
who rob them' (Ps. 35:9–10).

This capital will also be a great lever to release loans from commercial banks to finance agro-based industries and commerce such as dehydrating potatoes mentioned in Chapter 3. For unless some of the population that lives off agriculture is transferred to non-agricultural jobs, poverty cannot be eradicated.

   Please send your deposits to:

> INDIAN GROUNDWORK TRUST
> Reg. Charity No: 327770
> c/o Mr Prabhu Guptara
> 58, Ridgeway Road
> Farnham, Surrey
> England GU9 8NS
> Tel. 0252-713643

Those who may wish to send their money not as a deposit but directly as a grant to be kept as a revolving fund in India can contact the author. We are building up a company: Ashish Venture Capital and Consultancy for Development and Self-Employment.

> Bethany
> Landour
> Mussoorie, U.P. 248179
> India